Praise for
Opus Lux – How to Create Your Own Light

Opus Lux - How to Create Your Own Light is, in my opinion, the next breakthrough book about personal healing for this decade. Christa Rae Pacheco has written an exceptional handbook for healing the mind, body and soul that is worth its weight in gold. Opus Lux is astonishingly comprehensive, touches on all the nooks and crannies of our human experience and shows us how to adjust, balance and shift the current condition of our bodies, minds and souls. I sincerely believe that Opus Lux is a metaphysical masterpiece and should be required reading for everyone over the age of twelve.

Christa has synthesized a lifetime of study and gleaned every morsel of truth from some of the world's most stellar thinkers, philosophers, healers, teachers and writers; yet she has made the Opus Lux system distinctly her own. There is magic between the covers of her book and I heartily recommend it, and the processes she outlines, to anyone, anywhere who wants to change something about their bodies, their feelings and their lives. Personally, I could not put this book down. In fact, I only put it down to write this rave review. I'm going back to begin reading it again, starting with page one, just as soon as I finish writing this review.

I am excited for Christa about the publication of her work, but, even more so, I am positively thrilled for the people who buy it and are able to change their lives for the better with the information Christa has to offer. Every page contains a new thought, a radical way of reversing old thinking plus a torrent of fresh solutions for every issue imaginable under the sun. The processes are quick, effective and spiritually "green." I would buy this book again for the value I received on just three pages: P. 101, P. 129 and P. 135. The Chapter on "12 Commonly Believed Lies" is not only brilliant, but eye-opening and incredibly helpful.

Opus Lux is a real gem. I encourage everyone to treasure Christa and her work like the crown jewels. She's a teacher's teacher. Thank you Christa for this outstanding and critically needed work. It's already changing lives all over the world.

Kac Young DCH, RSM

My deeply embedded, unhealthy belief systems had trapped me in a life where I lived to serve others and ignored myself and my needs to the point where I no longer had a desire to live.

Christa Pacheco has an extraordinary gift. I'm very pleased to report that

the wisdom and insight she so graciously shares in Opus Lux - How to Create Your Own Light has transformed my life from one filled with pain and self-doubt to one filled with joy and a strong sense of well-being.
Ivy Coelho

"Christa's philosophy and her work were life changing for me. For the first time in my life I gave myself permission to say "No" to all the obligations that were leading me to a slow, painful death and "Yes" to all the healthy things I needed to do to bring life back to my tired body and joy back to my overburdened soul. At 55, after a lot of work, I'm living the life I was meant to live and am more productive than ever before!"
Karen Grencik, Literary Agent

Accurate and penetrating deep down to the core of my being, has been my experience each time I have entered into the world of Opus Lux. Blocks and blind spots unveiled. I have found the insights profound for my personal soul journey. Where there have been blind spots in my being -- now there is clarity.
Diana DeGarmo, Astrologer

The Opus Lux philosophy has taught me to recognize the "gift" in my "lessons", and then to be grateful for it so that my soul can move on to new experiences of a higher vibration. I have had wonderful compliments from friends who have observed the effects of my new behavior and soul-energy.
Blessings of Gratitude,
Deborah Krueger, Author of "Let's play Gratitude!"

Changing my perspective has been a journey that I intend to brighten every day. Every time I feel I don't know the answer "Opus Lux" reminds me I ALWAYS do. I feel everyone should have a copy of "Opus Lux" in their home. The understanding this book brings is huge. It will help transform lives one after another. Having this information brings me closer to myself, loved ones and our beautiful earth!
Ashli Woodgrift

Opus Lux

How to Create Your Own Light

A powerful, cutting-edge guide to creating perfect balance for your physical, mental, emotional and spiritual well-being

Christa Rae Pacheco, Medical Intuitive

Published by
Opus Lux DNAScan Seminars
P.O. Box 2856
Pismo Beach, CA 93448
www.ChristaRaePacheco.com

Christa Rae Pacheco.
Opus Lux – How to Create Your Own Light / 1st edition

Prepared for publishing by: Karen Grencik, Literary Agent
www.redfoxliterary.com

Cover & interior design, painting, illustrations: Darko Janevski, Graphic Design www.aimlessfly.com

Portrait Photo: Scott Gantenbein & Lynn Parks, Mindseye Multimedia Studio
www.mindseyestudio.com

ISBN-13 9780615519852
ISBN-10 0615519857

Printed in the United States of America

~ My Deepest Appreciation ~

It was most certainly divine intervention to have come across the many mentors, teachers, guides, friends, and supporters in exactly the order and with the perfect timing they appeared in my life. Thank you to everyone who has played a role in my unfolding. You are greatly appreciated and loved.

~

I especially would like to thank Marc Allen, Margaret Ruby, Neale Donald Walsch, Caroline Myss, and Louise Hay, all bestselling authors who have inspired me and led me to take the pieces I found in their teachings, add what my own inner knowledge and higher Guidance offered, and put them together in ways no one has before, to derive the gold, and create a cutting-edge formula for Self-healing designed for the 21st century.

~

Hans-Peter Zimmermann, Wayne Dyer, Anthony Robbins, and Lee Carroll, who started me on my own quest for personal and spiritual development and who gave me the first inkling of just how powerful our beliefs are.

Nikola Tesla, a true visionary far ahead of his contemporaries, whose life inspired me to think outside the box and follow through, no matter what others were saying.

~

Karen Grencik, who passionately midwifed the birth of this book and poured her heart and Soul into the promise and satisfaction of a successful delivery. She dedicated her time and expertise to clean up my baby until it glowed and I am eternally grateful to this kind-hearted Angel on Earth.

My two dearest friends, Amanda Smith and Barbara Brundege, who are both amazing healing facilitators and who have cheered me on, believed in me, shone light on my darkest moments of doubt, and are forever cherished for their surefire, passionate, unceasing support.

~

And finally a ginormous love-filled thank you to my treasured family: My beloved Dad who has been acting as my guardian angel for well over 40 years, Mama Rosy for her willingness to play her roles so well, and her ability to change at an incredible pace at an age when others are ready to give up. My sister Anita, for her undying support and generosity, to my sister Remy, for showing me what true courage is, and my brother, Dani, who was my best friend and whose spirit visits to bring important information from the other realm.

To my husband, Tim, who serenades me with his beautiful guitar music and who freely shares his incredible love with me; to Jessy my free spirited, gifted artisan daughter who is creative beyond measure; to Mikey, my luminous, peaceful son who will bring awesome change to the world; their Dad Rene, for being a true friend and the best storyteller of all; to Holly and Kerry, my much loved, artistic, winsome stepdaughters for taking me into their hearts and allowing me to be part of their lives, and to the entire Pacheco clan for inviting me seamlessly into the fold of a family I never had in this country.

You all are the cause and effect, my deepest source of inspiration and my greatest blessing.

Hymn to Isis

For I am the first and the last
I am the venerated and the despised
I am the prostitute and the saint
I am the wife and the virgin
I am the mother and the daughter
I am the arms of my mother
I am barren and my children are many
I am the married woman and the spinster
I am the woman who gives birth
And she who never procreated
I am the consolation for the pain of birth
I am the wife and the husband
And it was my man who created me
I am the mother of my father
I am the sister of my husband
And he is my rejected son
Always respect me
For I am the shameful and the magnificent one

Third or fourth century BC,
discovered in Nag Hammadi, Egypt

~ Preface ~

"Remember, you are never given a wish,
without the power to make it real."
~Author unknown~

Welcome, and congratulations! You have just given your Self the power to turn your wishes of health, abundance and happiness into reality. Does this sound impossible to do on your own? Or that it will take forever to accomplish? Well, let's take a moment to examine those beliefs.

There is a secret to transforming your dreams into reality. It is very simple. And once you hear more about it, you may be surprised by how well you already understand the way it works. What you are experiencing in your life, whether it be perfect health or physical pain, is created by how you feel.

Your perspective creates your attitude. Your attitude creates your beliefs. Your beliefs create your behavior. Your behavior creates how you feel. How you feel creates your reality. Do you really truly love your reality? Or would you like to change your perspective and begin to create a balanced, loving relationship with your Self, to affect your physical body, the interactions with the people in your life, the flow of money, Mother Earth and everything on it?

No matter what you wish for, you can create it with ease and grace. And even if your life is currently filled with pain, devoid of beauty or abundance, now is a good time to start. Following the steps in this book, no matter where you are, will allow you to become more and more of who you truly are. You will learn that it's okay to be good to your Self, to respect your Self, and to ask others to treat you in the manner you desire.

If I can do it, YOU can do it! It has taken me forty-some years, hundreds of Self-help books, innumerable hours of meditation, studying under Master Teachers, and working with thousands of individual clients to come to the insights that have helped me to overcome my own limiting beliefs and have allowed me to create the life of my dreams.

My passion for digging deep to find the root cause of imbalance has allowed me to cleanse away all unnecessary "fluff" and get right down to what works. It is this passion that has given me the tools to create my own amazing health, wealth and happiness, and there is no greater joy for me than to share these hidden treasures with you. Live life to the fullest!

Contents:

Introduction.. 1
Recollections of Childhood.. 3
Journey into Adulthood.. 8
Revelation.. 12
Everything is Energy.. 27
Good Vibrations.. 29
Chakra 101.. 34
Meridians – Pathways of Chi.. 43
DNA Scan for your Emotional Body.. 51
2012 – End Times? 57
Old vs. New Human Energy.. 61
Living My True Life's Purpose.. 68
Inner Male meets Inner Female.. 73
Basic Needs.. 78
Responsibility.. 82
Nurturing.. 87
Acceptance.. 96
Forgiveness.. 101
Relationships.. 108
Swiss Cheese.. 115
The Power of Words.. 119
12 Commonly Believed Lies.. 129
Manifestation.. 130

~ Introduction ~

"Our moments of illumination are like diamonds twinkling atop
a moonlit sea, reflecting a light that emanates from
a source far beyond the world it bathes."
~YON~

What does Opus Lux stand for? Opus translates to Create, and Lux means Light. So, what exactly is Opus Lux? For some, Creating Light will mean having a clearer understanding of who they really are. For some it means shedding their old skins and becoming more true to themselves. For many it will lead to balanced relationships, a fulfilling vocation, financial freedom, a healthy body, positive thinking patterns, emotional cleansing, and spiritual awareness from here forth, and to its fullest potential, on an ever evolving spiral. And for some it will mean all of the above, as well as learning to shine the light on themselves, becoming more nurturing, loving, kind, generous, compassionate and joyful towards their own Self.

Creating Light is a perspective, an attitude, a belief, a behavior and a feeling that begins with a willingness to change and ends with the reward to draw to your Self anything that you desire!

Since Opus Lux revealed itself to me, I have been able to discover my Self-worth. I learned how to trust and whom to trust, to truly forgive, to communicate my feelings and emotions, to create beautiful lasting relationships, to know when letting go is appropriate, to heal physical and psychological wounds, and how to love my Self and stand in my own power.

Once you read my story and the examples from my practice, it will become clear to you that other people's struggles and challenges are similar to yours. There are answers and solutions that lead to actions which will create a different consequence and a more desired result than you may currently be experiencing.

Little did I know what life had in store for me when I first heard the term "Medical Intuitive" in 1998. Caroline Myss, who is a famous pioneer in bringing awareness to the Medical Intuitive profession, described it as someone who can "read" a person's internal physiological condition intuitively, rather than by physical examination and diagnosis. I felt a kinship with her since I have always been able to intuitively "read" a person's emotional, mental and physical condition, "seeing" which beliefs create the behavior that creates the feeling that creates a seemingly unchangeable physical reality. This reality may include pain, hardship, suffering and limitation in health, relationships, career and abundance.

You live in a world filled with potential – potential to create your desired reality, a life filled with ease and grace, incredible health, fulfilling relationships, purpose-driven vocations and overflowing abundance.

It has been my mission and my Soul's purpose to give you everything you could possibly need to empower your Self to create your desired reality. Now you can heal your Self, on your own, in your own space, with an amazingly simple, yet exceedingly powerful, cutting-edge method. The ingredients are derived from Highest Source, through ancient wisdom, "secret" shamanic teachings, Higher Knowing and modern day Master Teachers.

All have undergone thorough analysis, testing on humans, animals, plants, and represent a breakthrough in the science of modern energy medicine. The last 30 years of my life have been spent acquiring metaphysical knowledge, using my analytical abilities to weed through massive amounts of information to find the gold, and then applying my genuine mind to put it all together, creating alchemy in a new and exciting way.

Once you change your perspective, your attitude changes. When your attitude changes, your behavior changes. When your behavior changes, you feel different. It is the feeling that creates your reality. Allowing change into your life leads you into the Promised Land and opens the gate to the new Golden Age of Higher Consciousness, creating a world of balance and living and Being as who you truly are—a Light-Being having a physical experience.

~

It is my desire to help you realize that you are Divine, connecting you to the potential, as well as the responsibility, this knowledge may hold.

Opus Lux Action Tip

Ask your Self if you give your Self permission to heal. It is you that is healing you! Giving your Self permission to heal means you are willing to change.

~ Recollections of Childhood~

"The highest reward for a person's toil is not what they get for it, but what they become by it."
~John Ruskin~

Each person holds their own truth. By sharing my truth and my philosophy, I invite you to only take from it what resonates with your own Inner Knowing and leave the rest behind.

My Story

Growing up in the heart of Europe sounds desirable. My homeland is best known for its neutrality, cheese made from milk derived from alp-going, bell-bearing cows, supremely crafted chocolates, precision-built clocks and watches, vaulted banks with guarded secret accounts, majestic snow-covered mountains and yodeling folk-singers. My family lived in a modest home near the town of Bern, Switzerland, which, from a bird's eye view, looks like an island, safely entwined by the Aare River.

My dad, I was told, was a brilliant inventor who had worked for an elevator manufacturer, was exposed to asbestos at work, and passed away after a long battle with lung cancer when I was four years old. He was our provider and nurturer and had been the one who truly desired to have children. My father used to play the accordion, and I remember sitting on his lap, while having no memory of being held in that way by my mother.

She had grown up in Germany during World War II with her mother and grandmother, both demanding and indifferent to a child's needs for affection and nurturing, and a father who, upon his return from service, had become cold and unpredictable. My grandmother finally decided to leave grandpa and moved herself and her own by now grown children back to Switzerland. My mother had successfully graduated from an apprenticeship as a gardener and a florist, which brought out her amazing creativity as a master in a craft that she flourishes in to this day.

My mom and dad had met fairly late in life, and I was told, and found it romantic, that they had gotten engaged on top of the Matterhorn in the Swiss Alps.

~

My older sister was born nine months after their wedding and was almost six years old when our dad died. She was told that "He is with the angels now," and then swiftly punished for being excited and happy for him. He had left no savings or life insurance, and my mother resolved to open her own flower shop to create income and put her talents to use.

Unfortunately, she had limited skills in effectively building and running a successful business, and was completely overwhelmed with the task of providing for a family all on her own. Before too long, she had given her trust to the wrong man and gotten her Self into debt. The debt was so extensive that no regular person could ever work it off, even if they worked hard for the rest of their life.

Being afraid of what people might say if she failed to pay restitution, my mom opted against filing for bankruptcy. She also had a great desire to keep her business and prove her Self. It became her obsession to pay back all that she owed, expecting that everyone, including her employees, us kids, and later even some of our friends, work hard, while over time, she grew increasingly more demanding.

Life offered my mom the opportunity to rescue a set of twins from extreme dire straits. The role of being a foster parent brought in a small amount of much-needed money, but it also increased her already considerable load. She completely overworked her Self, became a screaming banshee, abusive, and throwing violent temper tantrums. She lost touch with reality and developed severe asthma attacks, which led to problems with her reproductive and digestive systems. She was no fun to be around, for sure.

~

Feeling exploited and abused, I started craving affection and positive attention. I have always felt that I was starved of the love, kindness and nurturing a child deserves. Sitting on my bed in the dark of the night, I asked God why I was treated with so much indifference. Was I not deserving, or too unworthy, to receive just a little bit of warmth? I was literally freezing cold all the time and God appeared uncaring and seemingly never answered my questions.

In Sunday school, and in preparation for confirmation into the Reformed Church of Switzerland, I soon had questions for the priest that made him squirm and resort to the doctrines prescribed. He recited, that indeed, what the church taught had to be taken literal and that none of the stories in the bible were to be seen as metaphors. God was outside of us, judgmental and wrathful and to be taken seriously—giving the institution a stronghold on its followers. Jesus was the only son of God, and the rest of us were deemed weak and insignificant, just sheep following the Shepherd.

None of this ever resonated with me. Later I discovered, and was drawn to metaphysical concepts, and found more and more hypocrisy and incongruence in the teachings of my religious upbringing. I started exploring different religions, looking for something that fit me and felt true to my heart.

~

School proved to be a formidable challenge. I rebelled against authority figures and refused to do homework I did not understand. There was no help with school assignments at home, and it was easier to claim I lost my traditional red leather backpack than to admit that my busy mom had no time to sit down with me and explain math.

I had virtually no friends until I entered sixth grade, and I was ridiculed by my schoolmates for poor hygiene and wearing the outdated hand-me-downs found in my aunt's attic or the itchy hand-knitted wool leggings, skirts and sweaters created by my well-meaning but stern grandmother.

Everyone in my class seemed to have loving, caring parents, nice warm clothes, a safe, clean home, and, unfathomable to me, free afternoons to play and be a kid. Observing them filled me with jealousy and rage. I clearly remember once, on a particularly gray day, walking up to a privileged girl who was relaxing comfortably on her back on a cement step in the contemporary courtyard of my new secondary school. I grabbed her by her luscious, well- groomed hair and pushed her head down on the hard surface below her.

Anger stuffed down over a long period of time had found a target. She probably never quite understood what had brought on this attack, and never told on me. Please forgive me, my fellow fifth-grader. Looking back, I now understand why it happened, but am truly shocked, embarrassed and appalled by my cruel behavior.

The blessed first day of seventh grade brought me the fortune of a gifted teacher who I will forever treasure. He deeply cared for each and every one in our class, and guided and taught us over the next three years to become aware of our gifts, leaving me filled with hope for a better life and inspired to open my heart. Thank you, great, wonderful teacher, for your love and for giving me a reason to go on!

~

Truly stepping into her masculine power, my older sister demanded that I become as strong as she was. Her inner warrior was brought out often and clashed with my usual conflict-avoiding, will-create-peace attitude. It was my job to calm everyone down, hide to avoid the forthcoming blows, and hers to drive an angry fist through a reinforced glass door in rebellion of being locked in.

Adding two foster kids to our family dynamics gave both my sister and me an opportunity to gain a friend and an ally that was safe and welcomed. They became brother and sister. And even though this meant sharing what little there was, we had fun playing, singing and dancing karaoke style, in unison to the theme song of the then popular Bonanza TV show, drinking my mom's liquor in tiny sips, and floating next to each other on small water rafts on the billowing ocean on our trips to Yugoslavia or Italy.

These yearly trips to the open waters of the ocean were done on a shoestring, filling me with a sense of adventure, freedom and expansion. Imagine my stressed-out, oblivious mom, smoking up a storm in the cramped, windows up or else you're in trouble French-built car, with four kids gasping for air, on her way to a destination where she could relax for a few days and forget her own misery. Staying in cheap, privately-owned family pensions, drinking strong Turkish coffee served by their eldest in the dawn of morning, and then spending the day under the warm rays of the sun, swimming, floating and diving for shells in clear, turquoise water are the best memories of my childhood.

~

Being part of my mother's nature club exposed me to an elderly, slimy and predatory pedophile. When I told her about his unwanted, disturbing advances, I was told to come up with something different to get her attention. I experienced additional, although less intrusive, sexual advances from male neighbors, and never told a soul, thinking it was pointless.

At the blooming, but lonely, age of thirteen, I got "attention" from a man seven years older than me who took full advantage of my youthful trust and vulnerability.

Finally, shortly before I turned sixteen, I fell madly, deeply and unconditionally in love with a beautiful, unique and sensitive man four years my senior. To my great surprise, that love was miraculously returned, and for the first time in my life I felt unconditionally loved, cherished and adored! I was in heaven, wearing pink shades, and soaking up every morsel of love that was so freely given to me. It was love at first sight, and in my enthused, youthful exuberance, I never for a second doubted that we would spend the rest of our lives together.

Unfortunately, and very naturally, since we were still very young, three years into our relationship he fell in love with someone else and left me with a shattered, broken heart. I did my best to hide the ensuing pain that was literally bringing me to my knees, turning my pillow into a wet, feathery mass at night, feeling like my whole being was dying, and deeply afraid of never finding again what I had lost. Recovery was slow and arduous, and my life seemed meaningless and empty once again. Is it really better to have loved and lost than never to have loved at all?

~

According to Swiss-folklore, the profession you choose, after you graduate from high-school, is supposed to sustain you for the rest of your life. Having only one chance to pick which direction to take, was very scary.

At the tender age of fifteen, I began a four-year apprenticeship as a display artist. Working within the framework of an established commercial atelier, under the tutelage of a seasoned professional, allowed me to break away from my mother's business, and gave me a creative outlet.

I met the mysterious, austere and hauntingly beautiful young woman that would become my best friend in Bern at the Art College we both attended. Since our apprenticeship salaries were minimal, we earned extra money by offering our decorating skills at trade shows, which allowed us to travel and go out on the town. Planning to travel to far-away, exotic-sounding Australia to visit my friend's older brother after graduation gave me the necessary energy to handle a demanding work situation, and also served as a welcomed distraction to the seemingly never-ending grief and silently torturing mourning of the loss of my first true love.

I could not wait to get away from home and leave all the craziness of my life behind.

Opus Lux Action Tip

Write your own short version of your personal autobiography to discover the important pieces of your life's story.

~ Journey into Adulthood~

"Then the time came when the risk it took to remain tight in a bud was more painful than the risk it took to blossom."
~Anais Nin~

Shortly before my twentieth birthday, which officially turns Swiss citizens into legitimate adults with all common rights and responsibilities, I was unaware of how what happened next would affect my life. I was playing a game of eight ball with my girlfriend when I met the man that would become my first husband and exceptional father of my two amazing children. He was an expert pool player, interestingly different than anyone I had met before, refreshingly eccentric, and had already spent a few years traveling and living in America as well as in Australia.

If you know the song "Freebird," it perfectly describes him, and I was utterly fascinated by this adventurous, worldly Being. The promise of a new start with someone so carefree and experienced was indeed tempting. We dated for a few months before I decided to join him in his enticing plans, packed my red lacquered suitcase, had my hair braided in tiny rows, and moved to the United States. I left my family, my friends, and my plans to travel to Australia behind.

It was terribly exciting and, although I did not speak any English, I was thrilled to meet my boyfriend's friends and move into their already cramped, dark-wood-paneled, high-pile-carpeted, single-wide mobile home on the Central Coast of sunny California.

A few weeks later we rented an all-green decorated room at the very low friend rate of seventy-five dollars a month in a big square house right on the beach. It was exciting to travel all over the country in an old gold-colored station wagon, which we traded for a well-used pick-up with a camper shell before roaming Mexico's white sandy beaches for an incredible three months. We happily lived off fish harpooned by ambitious fellow campers, and later explored the economically diverse, picture perfect Caribbean.

~

The Central Coast became our true home, and we decided to return here after going back to Switzerland to obtain a work visa, get married, and welcome our tiny, beautiful daughter into our lives.

Upon our much anticipated return to The States, we opened a rapidly growing travel service with a rental fleet for Swiss tourists on a low budget, too young to rent from the competition, or with plans to travel for an extended period of time. Buying used cars, mini-vans, campers, motor homes and motorcycles, and repairing, cleaning and fixing them up, was just part of the services we offered. Dealing with the bureaucracy of corporate America, untangling red tape, paperwork, and being there for our clients required our full attention and provided for an overwhelming workload.

Living in close quarters with our young daughter, a brand-new baby boy, and a never-ending stream of guests created a life that was filled with parties, cleaning, cooking, cleaning, outings to the lake, cleaning, and everything else that comes with a house filled with family, friends, friends of friends, and people that had heard of us somewhere, and left me deeply yearning for privacy, quiet, and a clean house.

A vacation with just my husband and kids, or a romantic dinner without him spontaneously driving from our country barn home into town to sell one of our used fleet cars to a local, was as rare as a seared steak. He loved all the activity, while I started to slowly die.

Doing the alchemy on why our thirteen-year marriage ended, if I was asked to put it in a nutshell and had only one word to describe the reason, it would boil down to ignorance. In the midst of all these people, I felt utterly and completely ignored. For all these years I had made sure that everyone around me had everything they could possibly need, and I was absolutely spent.

I begged my husband for change, to limit the number of guests, to focus on us, to move to town, to explore different business options, to go to marriage counseling for more than four sessions. He was happy with how things were and had no need for change. I finally understood and knew deep down that I had to leave and take care of my Self to survive.

Breaking the news to the kids proved to be the most heart-wrenching task, the saddest moment in our life together as a family. The rhythm of their lives was disrupted, and the sense of security ripped from under them. Going back and forth between parents became a weekly ritual, and after the initial shock, our children displayed an enormous capacity to adjust and thrive regardless.

~

A no-down-payment mortgage helped me to buy a modest new home in town, something that I had been pining after for many years.

Over the previous year I had taken all available classes at the local massage school, initially to escape into a calm sanctuary, and with the only intention being to enhance my own technique used to relieve my husband's stress. Eventually those skills provided me with the income I needed to put food on the table and a roof over our heads. With no child support or alimony payments, no savings of my own, I started building my own business. Until I redirected my energy, I squeezed small portions of the money from the business we had built together and had been promised in the divorce proceedings from my generally generous, yet notoriously frugal ex-husband.

I loved my new space for all it provided. It felt like true luxury because everything was shiny and new. There was a door on my bedroom, which we hadn't had when we lived in the barn. I felt I finally had the time to be a better mom to my kids, cooked dinners for the three of us, and thoroughly enjoyed my quiet meditations, the absence of TV noise, and the joyful contentment of being alone. Envision me curled up next to our little dog in front of a fire that needed only the flip of a switch to engulf us in radiating warmth, blissfully oblivious for long moments to the pressures of the outside world.

~

After renting and sharing small offices for my massage business with others, my current roommate agreed to become my business partner, but left a few months after the grand opening of our own beautiful healing center. This left me owing the main portion of the money borrowed for construction and furnishings. I ended up filing for bankruptcy after a four-year struggle, and closed the center another four years later to pursue using my resources to create the writings you are holding in your hands.

While all the above was happening, my inner gifts developed more and more rapidly, and as I became comfortable with sharing the information that came to me from Higher Knowing, my expertise shifted and my treatments morphed from massage to energetic balancing and to the practice of being a Medical Intuitive, teaching Energy Medicine and Self-empowerment, as well as my own unique spiritual philosophy to individuals and groups.

~

In the meantime, and only after savoring plenty of alone time, I started looking for a new mate. My children were still hoping that their mom would return to their dad and at first greatly resisted the idea of allowing the handsome, tall, bearded stranger I had invited for dinner into their lives. We had met through a mutual friend and I was drawn to his gentle manner, dry humor, and his ability to evoke the most beautiful, melodic music from his guitar. It wasn't long before he also won the love of my kids, as well as the friendship of their dad.

Selling the house and moving into a rental with the man who would become my second husband eight years later came naturally, and it felt like we were doing a reality show on reenacting the famous Brady Bunch. Blessedly, all four of our combined children as well as our cat and dog got along splendidly, and the kids eventually and gradually moved out on their own. Today all of our children come home to visit, to eat a meal together, wash some clothes, or to spend a weekend or holiday with us.

~

I finally live the life I've always dreamed of. I am completely at peace with everything that has ever happened, and am absolutely grateful to everyone that has participated in my life experiences. Without them, I could never have gained the insights, the knowledge, the divine wisdom I am about to share with you. I am eternally grateful to each Soul, for each moment in this glorious world of duality, and to all that have supported my desire to live my purpose, as well as to all who have tried to hold me back, silence me, or offered an invite to spiritual warfare—which I always politely decline. Imagine there is a war and no one shows up *;-).

Opus Lux Action Tip

Identify the main characters in your life and write down what you love about them and what most annoys, irritates or bothers you about them. This will help you to figure out what part inside of you needs healing. How to utilize this concept is further explained in the following chapter.

~ Revelation ~

"May you know, without any doubt, the precious gift that you are.
And may you know the welcome of a presence
so loving that all fear subsides."
~Michael Still~

The two most important things I learned after moving to California were how to speak English and how to meditate. Meditation opened the gateway to a whole new enlightened world. All of a sudden I was connected to Highest Knowing of the Highest Source! I received amazing answers to my questions, and soon became aware of a host of energy Beings in the form of guards, guides, angels, teachers and others from the other realms.

I always ask that any information that comes through be of the Highest Good, Highest Truth, and of the Highest Source available. The information is usually extremely simple, easy to understand, and deeply resonates with me.

I am not channeling an entity like Lee Carroll who channels Kryon or Geoffrey Hoppe who channels Tobias, and I used to feel deprived or inadequate in comparison. That is, until my Higher Guidance told me that channeling entities in the "old-fashioned way" is no longer necessary. And that instead of allowing a non-physical form, different from my own personal Soul energy, to take over my physical body, I was tuning directly into Higher Source, which is much easier on the physical body and provides information from a diverse Source.

So, no matter what the question is, I get an answer from Highest Source, unless the question is beyond our collective evolution, or not relevant to my own growth or the growth of clients or other life forms I facilitate for.

It's a lot like talking on a walkie-talkie via telepathic communication in which I receive spoken messages, visions of what looks like a movie on a screen, images of symbols, pictures, whole paragraphs of the written word, a single word, a color, or the distinct feeling of a specific emotion, feeling or state of Being. This information is then translated and interpreted into the sought-after message or answer to the posed question.

Sometimes the answers arrive in a more subtle form days after the question was posed. I may be drawn to a bookshelf, pick a "random" book, open it where it feels right, look down, and there is my answer. Other times I may ask a question, turn on the radio, and the lyrics of the song that is playing contains all I need to hear. There are answers to be had from our surroundings, and when we pay attention, we will find that everything is in divine order and in absolute synchronicity. A good amount of the information in this book, as well as the following dialogue with Higher

Source, started to come in with a visit from my mom. The messages continued to materialize regularly, adding more and more insights, and eventually all the pieces tied together.

~

My mother sporadically traveled from Switzerland to visit. On one of her visits, she lied and lied and lied. I asked her to stop lying and told her she could just be her true Self. She would not stop and defended her Self when confronted. I eventually got so angry with her that I slammed my fist on the table and yelled at her that I no longer tolerate liars in my house. She continued to defend her Self, and that night I meditated, connected to my Higher Guidance and said:

Okay, guys, I need to know why my mother is lying to me.

She's not lying "to" you, she is lying "for" you, which means we are asking you to step out of your Victim role.

I really don't know what that means. Would you please explain?

Okay, let me ask you this: Does God, Source, Higher Power, Allah, Brahman, whatever you may call It, know everything about It-Self?

I thought about this for a moment and then said: If He is supposed to have created all that is, and everything is so amazingly perfect, I have to assume that God knows everything about Him-Self.

"Knowing" and "Being" are two different things. Think about the time before you became a mom. You thought you knew what it was going to be like to be a mom. But then actually being a mom was completely different. When you were a passenger in a car before you ever drove a car, you thought you knew what it was going to be like to drive a car. And when you finally sat behind the wheel for the first time as the driver, it was very different, and you were overwhelmed with shifting gears, working the clutch, looking out for other drivers, while keeping an eye on the speedometer and all the other gadgets. "Knowing" is a concept, a theory, and "Being" is the practical application of the theory.

This Earth-plane was created by God so that She could be all that She knows She is. It was created within duality so that a lower vibration could be experienced and She could know who She is not so that She can experience contrast, an opposite, a difference, to know who She truly is.

Day and night, white and black, tall and short, sweet and bitter, manipulation and respect, control and freedom—everything positive and anything negative is created by God and is part of all that is.

Who am I, then, and how do I fit into this concept?

Have you ever seen a dead body? And if yes, what was missing?

Yes, it looked like an empty box, a shell, and the life force energy of the person, animal or plant was gone.

Where does the energy that animates your physical body when it is alive -- your Soul -- go when the body dies?

I had just read Elizabeth Kuebler-Ross' book on death and dying, where she wrote about the findings of research on people that had had a near-death experience. Of those who could consciously remember the event, what many of them had in common was that they were drawn to a brilliant light and that they felt completely immersed in an overwhelming sense of love.

I said: The Soul goes back to the light.

Where was your Soul before it incarnated into the physical form and into your body?

I don't know. I am not sure if it was created by Higher Source, or where my Soul energy has been in between lives, or where it has come from.

Imagine that your Soul lived in the light before it incarnated into your physical body. That this light is the highest vibration possible, and that it consists entirely of love, and that love is everything that feels good -- kindness, grace, freedom, honor, respect, security, compassion, abundance, honor, dignity, excitement, joy, enthusiasm, and everything else that feels positive or is a state of Being that feels positive, amazing or pure.

Christians would call the light "heaven" and Metaphysicians would call it "the non-physical realm."

Just like your body is made up of a gazillion little cells, the "light" is the metaphorical body of God. It is made up of a gazillion little Soul cells, and you are one of them. Imagine that you sat in this light before you came into the physical body you are in right now, and that you know everything and anything that has ever been, is and will be. You are the All Knowing, you are the Creator energy that created all that is, you know that you are One with all that is, and that you are immersed in love.

You sat in this light and you said: I know everything about my Self, and I know what it feels like to be honest – and yet, I realize that my knowingness is just a theory, a concept, and I would like to experience the contrast and difference to knowing what it is to be honest. I would like to incarnate into the physical realm of Earth and into the most complex physical form there is, which is the form of the human being, so that I can experience duality and a lower vibration. Is there another Soul cell that would like to incarnate into the physical realm of Earth with me and lie for me so that I can know what it truly means to be honest?

Imagine that your mother's Soul cell held up her metaphorical hand and said: I love you so much, I will be happy to incarnate into physical form alongside of you and lie for you so you can know what it feels like to be honest. And you can do me a favor, too. I know that I am One with all that is, and I know that I am immersed in love, and yet I really don't know what that truly means. So, once we are incarnate into physical form, will you please leave me behind and abandon me so that I can experience being separate and finally truly know what it means to be One with all that is? Will you please hate me so that I can know the difference and the contrast to being immersed in love?

Now imagine that your Soul cell said to your mother's Soul cell: I love you so much and I will be happy to abandon you and hate you. Just treat me accordingly, and I will be glad to give you the desired experience.

You then gathered all of your guides, guards, angels, and others from the non-physical realm that are called to help you with your experience in the physical realm and came up with the rest of your very complex plan. It was decided on, carefully planned, and those who were going to enter your life for a specific purpose were chosen in agreement and for everyone's Highest Good.

This plan for a return to Planet Earth always creates great excitement, and you could barely wait to start your journey.

Why do I not remember living in the non-physical realm before I incarnated into my physical body?

In order for you to truly experience duality, you had to lose all memory of what was before and what will be after. Heavy veils are drawn to ensure a successful outcome, so you will not remember that you are on stage playing a role. It must feel real. Otherwise, you would laugh at the other Souls that you have chosen to hurt you, to make you suffer and to cause you pain so that you can find out who you are not, and in turn know who you truly are. You are a powerful, intelligent and creative Light-Being having a physical experience.

Once you return to the non-physical realm, reenter into your light body, and come home, you will sit with the other Soul cells that participated in your experience on the plane of duality and you will lovingly slap each other on the shoulder and say to each other: You played your role so well, we all thought it was totally real. And you will be glad to have experienced the suffering, for now you truly know what it feels like to be compassionate. You will be honored to have experienced pain, for now you know what it truly feels like to be filled with joy and aliveness. You will be delighted to have been hurt by betrayal, for now you know what it truly feels like to trust your Self.

What happens after the planning stage, and when does the Soul enter into the physical body?

When the sperm meets the egg, the first sliver of your particular Soul cell ignites life. Gradually, little by little, slivers of your Soul cell come in and activate and animate more and more of your physical form. When you are born, and with the first breath you take, you breathe in the larger, remaining portion of your personal Soul cell. The brain filters down and lowers the vibration of your Soul cell so that it can stay in your dense physical body.

Your blueprint, all that you came here to do and experience, is imprinted into the chakra system. The chakra system is part of your mental, emotional and spiritual bodies, and functions like a data bank in your computer. It holds the files of your life, your purpose, talents, strengths, abilities and gifts. Who you are going to meet, and for what reason, are stored in there.

Your subconscious is the all knowing. It is the Source, the Creator, God.

It knows everything about you, and all that ever was, is or will be. It knows exactly what your plan is, why you are here in the physical realm, and It will send visions, ideas and dreams to your third eye to activate the implementation of your purpose here on planet Earth.

The unconscious is a part of you that you are not consciously aware of.

Imagine that each of your cells contains your DNA. Your DNA consists of two physical, visible chemical strands that are looped and look like a rubber band, and many more invisible-to-the-eye energetic strands.

Within the DNA strands are thousands of genes, each containing a form of expression; physical aspects like hair color, eye color, skin color, bone density, etc. Archetypes like the Dictator (Hitler) are in there, the Martyr (Mother Teresa), the Lover, the Teacher, the Victim, the Saboteur, the Rescuer, the Villain. There are emotions, feelings, and states of Being, patterns, beliefs, and literally anything else that is a form of expression.

Your consciousness only allows you to be aware of your immediate surroundings. The five physical senses of touching, seeing, hearing, smelling, and tasting, as well as your extrasensory perceptions of clairvoyance, clairaudience, clairsentience, intuition, and instinct, are all part of your consciousness.

Is my mom consciously aware that she has to lie for me?

No, it's an unconscious program.

Can I make it stop? It bothers me, and her behavior really annoys me.

Yes, you can make it stop.

How?

Stop feeding the dog.

What dog?

Imagine that there is a metaphorical black dog sitting at your mom's feet that has a collar on it that says: Lie for Christa – and she has to do that for as long as the dog is there. Once you stop feeding the dog, it will leave.

How am I feeding the dog?

You are feeding the dog with your negative emotions. The frustration, anger or rage that you send towards the perceived perpetrator is what feeds the dog. Even if you never say a word, simply by feeling or thinking about it feeds the dog. Have you ever noticed how drained and tired you feel after engaging in anger or any other negative emotion? It literally eats at your substance and lowers your vibration.

How do I stop feeling that way? I am not willing to just look away, pretend nothing is happening, or shove it under the rug.

We are not asking you to look away and pretend like nothing is happening. We ask that you take a really good look at your mom and tell us what you see.

You want me to judge her?

Just do it!

Okay. When I look at her, I see a liar.

What would you like her to be instead?

I would like her to be honest.

Are you honest?

I am brutally honest, because I really despise lying.

Did you know that being brutally honest hurts just as much as lying? You are here in the duality to know both sides, experience opposites, and then bring it into balance. Are you willing to learn how to become honest in a loving way?

Wow, I'm a bit embarrassed, because I was rather proud of my Self for my courage to be brutally honest, and yes, I am going to be mindful and learn to communicate being honest in a loving way.

Are you honest with others?

Yes, I really do my best. It is very important to me.

Are you honest with your Self?

Well, I can't be. Growing up, I felt that I never had what I needed, and now I am doing my best to give my loved ones everything they could possibly need. I promised my Self that I would create a different environment for my own family than I had when I was a kid. My mom always struck me as selfish and Self-absorbed, so I'm aiming to be Self-less and giving. I do things for others that a lot of times feel like an obligation or duty. But someday all I do for others will return to me. The more I give, the more I will receive. The more I do for others, the more will be done for me.

And is it working?

No. Maybe I haven't done enough yet, or given enough yet, to get something back.

The law of attraction has it that if you only give to others, only others will get. In order for you to receive anything, you have to make your Self part of the equation, and give to your Self first until your own cup overflows. What overflows is what you give to others. If everyone did this, we would have no cliff hangers or Victims in desperate need, and, therefore, no need for rescue.

When you do for others what they can do for themselves, you take away their power. Give it back! Instead of fishing for them, teach them how to fish for themselves. Have you noticed that you feel strong and powerful when you take on someone else's load, and after awhile it becomes a burden? The other person is supposed to get stronger and then take back what rightfully belongs to them, but can't, because you have taken not just the burden, but their power, as well. They remain weak and helpless, and all this does, is fill your need to be needed and useful.

It is NOT what you GIVE to others or what you DO for others that comes back to you! It is what you PROJECT from your Self that comes back to you. Outflow creates inflow.

If you are very generous with others but are a scrooge with your Self, your photon light will go out and announce to everyone in big letters:

Be miserly with me! And they have no choice but to treat you this way.

No matter how nice and supportive you are with everyone else, if you are mean with your Self, berate and judge your Self, your photon light will go out and announce in big letters: Be mean to me. Talk about me in a negative way and judge me.

Outflow creates inflow. You will receive from others exactly what you give to your Self. They will treat you, never failing, exactly the way you treat your Self!

When you are honest with your Self, they will be honest with you.

When you are considerate with your Self, others will consider you.

When you respect your Self, others will respect you.

When you support your Self, others will support you.

This does not mean that you can't be generous, considerate, kind, supportive, or respectful towards others. It simply means that you treat your Self with as much respect as you treat others. You are equally important and you equally matter. If you feel ignored and overlooked, it is because you ignore and overlook your Self.

Why are you not living your own purpose, and instead are investing all of your energy into helping others to live theirs? Stop and figure out what your own purpose is! If everyone did what they came here to do, everything would be done.

Look around you, give up all obligations, anything that does not fill you with at least some measure of joy, enthusiasm or excitement. Only choose what serves your own purpose. Be honest with your Self!

Look at your mom and say: Mom, thank you so much for showing me how not to be with my Self!

When you understand that the two of you sat in the light together and you asked her to please lie for you so that you could learn to be honest, not just with others, but also with your Self, and you thank her for showing you how not to be with your Self, you will be grateful instead of angry and the dog will go look for food somewhere else.

The agreement, the contract between you and your mom, will be fulfilled on that level and she will either stop lying for you or it will no longer bother you. In that event, you will know you are healed and have restored that part of your authentic Self.

When you can look at all that annoys, bothers or irritates you about a situation or others, and ask your Self what they are showing you on how not to be with your Self, you will understand in all ways how you have wronged your Self and how you have failed to love your Self.

If you are being manipulated, know that this is your invitation to learn to respect your Self and set personal boundaries and limits.

If you are being controlled, look closely at how you are limiting your Self, or robbing your Self of well-deserved freedom.

When someone opposite you is an aggressive warmonger, and you usually avoid conflict, know that you are on two polar extremes, and you are being asked to balance your response by becoming a little bit more like the other person. In this case, you would become more assertive and confront conflict by communicating your needs or desires in an honest and loving way while staying calm and firm.

When you like something or see a trait you admire in someone, it is tempting to become a little more like this your Self. Who wouldn't like to be more confident, courageous or Self-reliant? A new thought is that if you despise something or dislike a trait in someone, that this, too, is an invitation to become a little more like this your Self. If you have an aversion to brutality, you may be on the far opposite side. Are you way too nice and could you benefit from adding a dash of boldness to your negotiation tactics?

If you love it, become more like it. If you hate it, become more like it. This will balance your responses and return you to being who you truly are.

I'm afraid I'm going to lose my family's love and my friends are not going to understand what has gotten into me if I do this.

Look into your heart and see if this is really true. Your statement is based on fear and is the voice of your Ego. Open your seventh chakra, located at the crown of your head, and allow your subconscious to send a vision, an idea, to your sixth chakra, and use your third eye, your imagination, to envision a life in which you are honest with your Self, live your true purpose, fill your own needs first, respect your Self, and make choices and decisions that serve and please you. How does this look to you?

It looks great!

Now send this picture down to your fifth chakra, in the area of your throat, and listen to the two voices that pop up. One is your Male voice and the other is your Female voice.

Your Male voice also represents your EGO voice.

This most imbalanced aspect of the Male voice is based on FEAR and is the voice that will give you all the reasons why your brilliant idea is NOT going to work. It will say things like: It sounds really selfish to fill your own needs first. Your loved ones are going to abandon you if you no longer do for them what you have done in the past. Your friends will see how selfish you have become and are going to judge you.

You will instantly recognize it as the EGO voice by its loudness and by asking your Self: Is what I'm hearing in my HEAD based on FEAR? Send the Male voice to the sideline and slow down long enough to hear your Female voice.

Your Female voice also represents your TRUE voice.

In its most balanced aspect, the Female voice is based on TRUST, and trust is housed in your HEART. It will give you all the reasons why your brilliant idea is going to work just beautifully. It will say things like: Filling your own needs first is natural and ensures your own well-being. Your loved ones are going to learn to rely on themselves. This will empower them, and they will appreciate you for it. Your friends are going to be grateful to you for being an inspiring example. It will free them up to consider themselves a bit more, and they will no longer resent you for feeling that they have to give to you what they have and then depend on you to get what they need.

You will recognize it as your TRUE voice by its confidence and by asking your Self: Is what I'm hearing in my HEART based on TRUST? Always slow down long enough to hear this small, still voice tell you to listen to what is most natural for you, and not what is most normal, makes most sense, or is rational. Eliminate the fear-based Male voice and go with the traditional Ladies first!

If I'm hearing you right, I'm best off if I base my choices and decisions on my Heart voice?

Yes. When you listen to your Heart voice, you will always get an experience that shows you who you truly are; while should you fall into the trap of listening to your Ego voice, you always get an experience that shows you who you are not.

Finding out who you are not is essential to knowing who you truly are, so please forgive your Self for each instance you listen to your HEAD instead of your HEART and experience the side of duality that allows you to gain wisdom by making a mistake.

Is listening to my Heart voice all I need to consider to manifest a desirable outcome?

As soon as you have identified and heard the Heart voice, the fourth chakra, which is located in your heart space, will open. You are invited to check to see if your vision, your idea that looks so good and sounds so natural, also feels amazing.

If it feels exciting, joyful, and there is a good measure of enthusiasm present, the next door opens and your third chakra in your solar plexus area opens up and asks: Will what looks so good, sounds so natural, and feels so amazing empower me?

It is vitally important to make sure you determine if the decision to act on your vision or idea is empowering you; and for right now, just you alone.

Now imagine that the Ego got tired of sitting on the sideline and has snuck down to your second chakra, located below your navel, and is voicing its fear-based opinions loud and clear: What about your loved ones? They will not like this decision of yours. They depend on you, and you can't just look after your Self! And on it goes.

Do not believe that you have to diminish your vision, your idea, your dream, because others depend on you! Know in your heart that if it empowers you, it will empower everyone involved. Even if it initially hurts them, it is giving them an opportunity to grow and expand in unforeseen and far-reaching ways.

Can I just trust that I will have everything I need for whatever I choose?

After you choose and decide based on your inner Female's qualities, you invite your inner Male to the table and ask him to organize and plan with logic and reason.

Think about it this way: The left side of your body is your Female side.

It is connected to the right side of your brain and has, among other aspects, the qualities of being passive, receptive, intuitive, and having inner knowing, higher wisdom, creativity, ease and grace. The right side of your body is your Male side. The Male side is connected to the left side of your brain and has, among other aspects, the qualities of being active, giving, and using working, doing, planning, logic, rationality and sense to create. Combined, the two create synergy and spectacular results.

Have your inner Female make the choices and decisions based on how they feel, and then ask your inner Male to come and sit with her to come up with a sensible, logical plan, a rational approach on how to manifest the vision, idea, or dream into physical reality.

The inner Female may ask the inner Male to consider the following:

Is this the easiest, most graceful way, or can we create greater results with less effort?

When the two work hand-in-hand, magic happens.

It is the Male that then takes the vision, idea or dream out into the physical realm and acts on taking the steps to bring it into manifestation.

You can trust (inner Female) that you will always have everything you could possibly need for whatever you plan (inner Male).

To top it off, your inner Female gets to remind you to take steps that feel possible while the inner Male makes sure you do it within your own means. This will build trust. And eventually, as larger and larger steps are possible, you will manifest with more and more ease and grace, creating greater results with less and less effort.

How do I overcome my deep-seated feelings of low Self-worth so I can stop investing my energy into proving to others that I'm worthy and just know from within that I am worthy and deserving?

Imagine that you are made up of many pieces. Just like a puzzle, these pieces combined make up the whole picture of who you truly are and contain different content. One piece holds the energy of dignity, another one security, another safety, protection, power, Self-worth, respect, abundance, belonging, intuition, confidence, joy for life, freedom of expression, being heard, clarity, vision, connection, Self-reliance, Self-importance. The list is endless.

You are conceived with all the pieces of who you truly are perfectly in place. You are whole until you either give away one of your pieces or until someone takes one away from you. You also take from others, and others give their pieces to you.

This can happen as early as the moment when your own mom and dad became aware of your presence, when your physical body was only a tiny fetus growing and expanding into the miracle of living as a separate Being in a sometimes harsh environment. Maybe your arrival was a surprise, and this may have caused them to feel fearful over their ability to provide you with what you will need; hence, robbing you of feeling desired, and creating the first hole. The feeling of being a burden fills the empty space.

More holes are created as you spend time in the duality.

You lose your confidence when someone makes fun of you in kindergarten. Insecurity fills the hole.

You lose your trust as someone betrays you. Resentment fills the hole.

You lose your security as someone exposes your vulnerability. Instability fills the hole.

Eventually your energy field will look like Swiss cheese.

All that was lost is now outside of your Self, and that's where you go to try to fill up the holes, since they are screaming to be filled with what was once there and get rid of the pain that is filling them now.

You over-do and over-perform to gain acknowledgment and recognition from outside of your Self to get rid of feeling inadequate.

You please others to gain affection and kindness from outside of your Self to get rid of feeling unloved.

You provide for others in hopes of being respected and seen as competent from outside of your Self to get rid of feeling useless.

You have to work very hard to fill these holes from outside of you, and they seem to be bottomless pits. The fulfillment is fleeting, and the hole is empty again before you know it. You are frustrated over how much energy you spent to gain something that feels good for a moment but never sticks.

Imagine you are in need of a liver transplant. The physical body will reject a liver if it comes from an outside source. The donor has to be a very close match. And yet, even if the foreign liver is finally integrated into your body, you still end up taking anti-rejection medication for the rest of your life.

The same happens when you try to fill the holes in your emotional body from an outside source, except that your emotional body will spit the foreign "filler" out without hesitation. Hard-earned acknowledgment, recognition, respect, or anything else that is added from outside your Self never fills the hole for very long. It falls right through the bottomless pit, landing squarely on the ground. The empty space is once again screaming to be filled. You could take medications that mask the empty feeling by numbing your emotional body but make you feel disconnected, a hollow shell of who you really are. How exhausting, and what a waste of energy for everyone involved!

After you have discovered that others cannot possibly supply you with what you need, you finally resort to filling your Self from within.

You are kind and loving with your Self,
which rids you of feeling judged.
You are generous with your Self, include your Self, and make your Self a part of the picture, which rids you of feeling left out.
You value your ability to rely on your Self and cherish the feeling of security when you trust your own inner guidance, which rids you of feeling at the mercy of others.

The holes in your Swiss cheese start to disappear, and you are returning to becoming whole. Only you can fill your Self with what you've lost!

So, respect your Self, and thank the one that took respect away from you, because you now know what it felt like when it was gone and truly appreciate it upon its return. Only what you lose will have value and will not be taken for granted. You did not even know you had it until it was gone, and you appreciate it a thousand-fold upon its homecoming. Such is the power and one of the reasons for duality.

Observe and ask your Self questions like these:
Why do I expect others to provide for me?
Why do I steal away someone else's sense of security?
Why do I manipulate others to gain a sense of being respected?
Why do I rob power away from others by doing for them what they can do for themselves?
What have I spent energy on to retrieve what I lost from outside my Self?
What if I could just fill my Self by giving to my Self what I need and am looking for?
What am I missing?
What will I do with what eventually overflows from me?
What if everyone did this, how would the world and how we interact with others, animals and the environment be affected?

Everything and everyone, including your Self, would become whole. No need to sell out anymore. No more Victims, Heroes, Rescuers. A world where each individual takes full responsibility for their life, filling their own holes, needs and desires by claiming what is rightfully theirs until they overflow, pouring what overflows into a healthy environment and to others, to replenish, create balance and partake in splendid abundance.

Know that it is your choice to give your power, sanity or security away to others who are hunting to fill their own holes. Choose to fill your own instead of wasting your energy on stealing what you need from others. Share what overflows from you freely, and receive what overflows from others with gratitude and appreciation.

Thank you. I have a much better understanding of cause and effect. I can see why bad things happen to good people. It is needed to experience who we are and who we are not, and I can see a much larger picture now. I realize that, despite the veils or fog I am surrounded by at times, I am a powerful, intelligent, creative Light-Being having a physical experience. I understand why I really needed to be fully immersed in the illusion of being a Victim of others or circumstance. I am aware that I may have asked to be betrayed, lied to or disrespected, and that this is just a reflection of how I am treating my Self or what I have failed to do for my Self. I am mindful and have discovered what I have given to others or what others have taken away from me and will end the search party and return home to fill my own.

If I asked other Souls to cause me pain so that I can find the opposite of who I am, I can easily forgive them. I can forgive my Self for asking to experience and come to the planet of duality to discover who I am not, and I will celebrate the insight of having gained the immeasurable gift of knowing who I truly am.

We are honored to be of service and are here to assist you in all ways.

Thank you!

Opus Lux Action Tip

Learn to connect to your own Higher Knowing and your own Higher Guidance by listening to the Opus Lux "Tree Mediation" CD that was designed to complement this book.

~ Everything is Energy ~

""Reality is merely an illusion, albeit a very persistent one."
~Albert Einstein~

The solidity of the world reflected in touchable matter seems absolutely indisputable. Fixed things that you can see and touch, like your body or the chair you are sitting on the tree outside your window, all are reassuringly solid. Beginning with Albert Einstein, modern physics has irrefutably established that this solidity is a mirage, a tactile sensation, nothing but a sensory illusion.

~

Your body is made up of atoms. These atoms are particles that are whirling at lightning speeds around huge empty spaces, and the particles are not material objects. They are fluctuations of energy and intelligence in a huge sea of adaptable life force energy, spinning at varied rates of acceleration. The variation in speed and density is what causes the illusion of physically noticeable appearance of matter.

The body is 99.9999% empty space, and the 0.0001% that you perceive as matter is—guess what? Empty space! Matter is a brilliant apparition of our perceptual experience. As you establish this scientific fact, microscopically analyze and examine your very material-looking physical body, the closer you look, the sooner you will end up with—you guessed it—nothing.

As you dissect through the different layers of organs, tissue, cells, molecules, and atoms, and remove layer after layer until you get to the subatomic realm, all that remains are bundles of energy vibrations. It is the nerve receptors in the body that turn these energy vibrations into what we perceive as our tangible five senses of touch, sight, sound, smell and taste.

~

It becomes clear that the fundamental natural material of the universe is that it is not solid matter, liquid or gas, but empty space. An atom, which is the basic unit of matter, only looks like a solid dimensional object, but it is, in reality, a void. Born out of this emptiness, this void, this non-matter, the Source of life creates the entire universe, everything in existence, from space to energy to time to what appears as matter. Even a tiny speck of dirt, or anything else that has substance and is considered matter, has mass. Because it has mass, it exerts gravity. The law of gravity is a natural occurrence by which objects with mass attract one another.

~

Thoughts form in the mind, and, up until recently, science promoted the notion that the mind is a secondary phenomenon of the brain.

Among others, Bruce Greyson, MD, who is a professor of psychiatry and neurobehavioral science who specializes in research on near-death experiences, has found that the mind and brain are separate and that information is retained outside of the brain. Clinical evidence has shown that the mind lives on after the brain stops functioning.

The brain is the receiver, not the producer of consciousness!

Thoughts are determinable entities with measurable mass. Mass exerts gravity, and gravity pulls things to it. Thoughts create feelings and emotions, which also produce mass. When enough people think fear-based thoughts and feel fear-based emotions, the gravitational force of these thoughts and emotions becomes reality and has a measurable effect on the physical world. Shared experience, the blending of a vast number of people focusing on specific events, leads to a particular outcome in the physical world. Can we improve our physical world by thinking new empowering thoughts that will lead to more positive feelings and transform negative emotions to then create a more desirable reality?

Absolutely!

The more people who change their perspectives, their attitudes, their beliefs, and behaviors to life-affirming, positive intent, the sooner we will create the desired outcome of living in peace and abundance.

~

Energy vibrates at different rates from finer to denser. Thoughts have a finer vibration than words. A rock has a denser, slower vibration than a more easily destructible life form like the human or animal body. Where do you start and where do I end? Our interrelatedness and energetic connection is what makes us all One.

Nothing and no one is separate. We are all in this together. For better or worse, we are affected and changed by perceived external sources of energy such as thoughts, words, deeds, natural elements and time. We can use this amazing knowledge to send a healing thought uninterrupted across the Atlantic, or be affected by the motion created by a butterfly flapping its tiny wings in a far-away land.

Opus Lux Action Tip

Take a moment to reflect on the fact that the essential substance of the universe is a holographic illusion of matter, time and space. The world and everything on it is simply a projection that gives us the illusion of solidity, a foundation on which we can pretend to be separate and all alone.

~ Good Vibrations ~

"Let a man radically alter his thoughts,
and he will be astonished at the rapid transformation
it will effect in the material conditions of his life."
~James Allen~

Energy vibrates. The better you feel, the higher you vibrate. Feeling down will literally lower your vibration. The highest vibration possible is pure love, and love is anything and everything that feels good -- joy, kindness, compassion, abundance, generosity, enthusiasm, excitement, passion, faith, affection, recognition, etc.

On a scale where level one is the lowest vibration to level ten being the highest possible vibration, where do you vibrate right now? Have you just hit bottom? Is depression or worry keeping you at a level two or three? Or are you feeling really good and enjoy living on a vibrational level between six and eight? To raise your vibration, you have to raise your consciousness. To raise your consciousness, you have to become aware and mindful of what kind of consequences your actions, beliefs and attitudes create. It is a universal law that each action always has the exact same consequence and the exact same result. Scientific proof of this concept is established when the exact same environment, identical procedure and ingredients produce the exact same result over and over—which it does every time as long as the integrity is maintained. The slightest variation will create a somewhat different result, which, when exactly recreated, will always yield the exact same result. It is also a universal law that lower vibration has no other choice than to raise up to meet a higher vibration if this higher vibration is maintained. When you maintain a high vibration, you help to raise low vibrational energy in your immediate environment.

When 144,000 people on Earth can maintain a vibration of level nine most of the time, all lower vibrations have no other choice than to lift up and join those who are holding the high vibration in place.

If you already have a higher vibration, help those who are almost as high as you to raise and maintain their vibration, instead of pouring all of your energy into those who are way down, or only use you as a fuel station, never intending to change their habits or ability to do for Self no matter how needy they appear.

You have the power to affect thousands of people in your community simply by creating a life for your Self that is filled with happiness, laughter, nurturing, confidence, purpose and abundance.

Is it hard for you to stay in a good mood when one of your loved ones has to deal with disappointment, is mad at the injustices of this world, or has made choices that have adverse consequences?

Do you go down into the hole with them, lower your vibration to match theirs to show your compassion and be on the same level with them, so they will not feel abandoned or uncared for?

Or do you consciously remain safely at the edge of the abyss, lower the rope down to the one at the bottom of the pit, letting them know that you understand what they are going through and that you will help them come up when they are ready to do so, while trusting that if you keep your own vibration up, they actually have a better chance to recover faster and more effortlessly? If you knew that you attract the exact same vibration to you that you project from you, would you be more inclined to attain and maintain the highest possible vibration?

Meet Marie. She embodies an archetype. Her story has been told in many ways and from many sources. It feels like we all know someone just like her. She is your typical PTA mom, a dedicated soccer mom. She bakes cookies for Sunday church, and you can ask her for any favor. She'll be happy to be of service to her community and everyone in it.

One day Marie was driving down the freeway when she was cut off and killed by a sixteen-year-old freshman, who was later charged with reckless driving and vehicular manslaughter. Everyone asked, "Why her? She was such a good person, always of service to everyone in need, just the nicest, sweetest woman, and we don't understand how this could possibly have happened to her."

Had you looked at her vibration before she died, you would have seen that it was at a level four. Had you asked her, "Marie, you are vibrating really low. Are you unhappy, or what is going on?" she would have said, "I have ideas for a whole book inside of me and feel the urge to just stay home, work on the computer, and write all day, but I can't, because I'm supposed to be of service. Everyone keeps asking me for favors. I'm feeling resentful for having to do all these time-consuming chores for everyone, and I feel bad about that, too."

Had she known that this book would have reached 100,000 or more people with her unique message, and that this was how she was supposed to be of service instead of helping the 200 or so individual people in her community, she would have felt better, and this, would have raised her vibration.

The young man had had a fight with his dad over having bad grades, he felt deserted by his friends, and was also vibrating at a level four. A perfect match—like attracts like. Even though the two looked completely different from an outside view, they were attracted like magnets on that fateful day. Aside from vibrating at the same level, Marie had what the teenager was lacking. She was celebrated in the community, acknowledged and recognized for her efforts, while he was on the opposite end, not consciously aware of it, but in desperate need of a fix for what was missing in him.

~

Each feeling, each emotion, has a specific universal vibration that we unconsciously recognize and seek, usually from outside ourselves, if we have lost or given it away. Like vampires, we target those who have what we need and steal what isn't ours to fill our own gaping holes when we don't know how to fill them from within.

On an emotional vibrational scale from level one being the lowest to level ten being the highest possible, jealousy in its lowest form, for example, vibrates at a level two. If you can turn the emotion of jealousy into envy, you raise the vibration to a level five. Allow envy to motivate you to create for your Self what others already have and the vibration will go up to a level seven. By the time you are happy about having been inspired to manifest something great for your Self, rather than being upset that others have what was denied to you, you have raised your vibration to a level eight or even nine. Congratulations!

It is your choice to turn low vibrational emotions into high vibrational feelings. Turn craving into desire, and desire into being content with what is right at this moment, and, voila, your vibration has taken a major leap.

The Soul is miserable in a low vibrational energy field and longs to be immersed in the high vibrational sphere of love.

The experience of being who we are not is important. How else would we know who we truly are? How long does one have to remain in the low vibrational energy of negativity? Did you know that you actually have a choice, and that you can change your vibration level at any time you decide to?

When you feel abandoned or left out, raise your vibration by nurturing, caring for and including your Self.

When you feel judged, accept your Self exactly the way you are.

When you feel shame or guilt, decide what you would have done differently, forgive your Self, and apply your newfound knowledge at the first opportunity that arises.

When you feel stressed out, slow down long enough to clear your head so you can make choices that please and serve you even in the midst of chaos.

Would you be surprised that food which has been raised with love has a much higher vibration than food that has gone through hell? The cruelty of feeding cows bone meal made from other cows' bones, or corn rather than hay or grass, is atrocious. To keep them in tiny stalls, standing in their own filth, is something we are willing to overlook. It's what makes it cheaper to buy.

On top of this, the cows are poisoned with hormones and steroids. Later, the meat is treated with more chemicals, over-processed, frozen, and most of it is prepared by people that earn minimum wage and have no time or incentive to pour love upon the meal they are about to serve to unsuspecting consumers.

Junk food is exactly what the word means, according to Thesaurus.com: Garbage. You will feel attracted to it if you have a low vibration. Remember that you will crave food that has the same vibration as you do. Choosing food that has been treated with love will help raise your vibration and help you to feel great. When you buy more organic, free range, and "prepared with love" foods, the greater the selection will become. Ask if the vegetables and fruits at the farmers market are organic. "Oh, we only spray the blossom" is the same as rubbing formaldehyde all over your newborn's delicate skin!

Should you unexpectedly find your Self in a junk food restaurant, bless your meal, acknowledge the suffering the food has endured, and enjoy it as much as possible.

Raise your consciousness to raise your vibration.

Consciousness affects our reality. Masaru Emoto*, a Japanese Doctor of Alternative Medicine, has visually documented the molecular changes in water by taking photographs of frozen water droplets, magnifying them under a dark field microscope, and discovering many fascinating differences in the crystalline structure of water.

Clean, pristine mountain stream and spring water created beautiful geometrical crystals when frozen, while polluted or toxic water developed a distorted structure. In his study, Emoto discovered the effects of human vibrational energy, thoughts, words, ideas, and music on the molecular structure of the true nature of water. Just like Mother Earth, you are made up of more than 70% water.

What does YOUR crystal look like?

Water, by the way, is the one natural element that has the ability to hold the highest vibration. In a time when the vibration on Earth is in need of rising, and since we've polluted our natural environment, is it really that perplexing that our glaciers are melting to create a platform of pure surface water to hold the high vibrational energy currently generated by all humans who are raising their consciousness?

* Masaru Emoto: See these truly astonishing water crystal photographs in "The Hidden Messages in Water."

Opus Lux Action Tip

You can practice maintaining a high vibration by being mindful of your choices and by becoming aware of how you respond to what is happening in your life. What seems like a tedious task of observation and analyses will become a habit and reward you with the ability to attract higher vibrational manifestations.

~ Chakra 101 ~

"The voyage of discovery is not in seeking new landscapes,
but in having new eyes."
~Marcel Proust~

The physical body contains systems like the respiratory or cardiovascular system; while the energetic bodies contain energetic (invisible to the physical eye) systems like the chakra and meridian systems.

"Chakra" is a Sanskrit word that means "wheel" or "vortex." Chakras are energy centers located in our immediate and extended energy field. The lower seven chakras are located along the physical form, interpenetrate the body, and are an interconnected system (see diagram). Number eight hovers about two to three feet above your head and is connected to both the lower and higher chakras that expand into the non-physical realm.

Look at them as if they were databanks in your computer, each of them containing files about your life. Imagine that each chakra was imprinted at birth with your personal blueprint for this particular incarnation.

~

Before entering your physical body at birth, your personal Soul cell traveled through the universal planetary system, the matrix of astrological signs, and along the way picked up energy, characteristics, and archetypes related to the planned experiences you have encountered ever since you arrived. With the first breath you took when you were born, all information in your blueprint was installed into your chakra system, and every aspect was organized and filed away into the appropriate chakra.

Since you do not consciously remember your personal blueprint, life unfolds in a never-ending string of pleasant as well as seemingly unwelcomed events, exposing you to complex variations of feelings and emotions. Even so, be assured that your all-knowing subconscious is a grand master and directs the events in your life with great skill and wise foresight.

~

Chakras absorb universal life force energy. In the northern hemisphere, they spin in a clockwise direction when they absorb Highest Source energy and in a counterclockwise direction when unneeded energy is returned to Source. When an imbalance occurs in one of your chakras, it can shut down, stop spinning, and close off. Aspects of your physical, mental, emotional or spiritual body within the vicinity of a particular chakra are affected and start to show symptoms of imbalance or disease when you fail to listen to your truth, guidance, and ignore your inner alarm system.

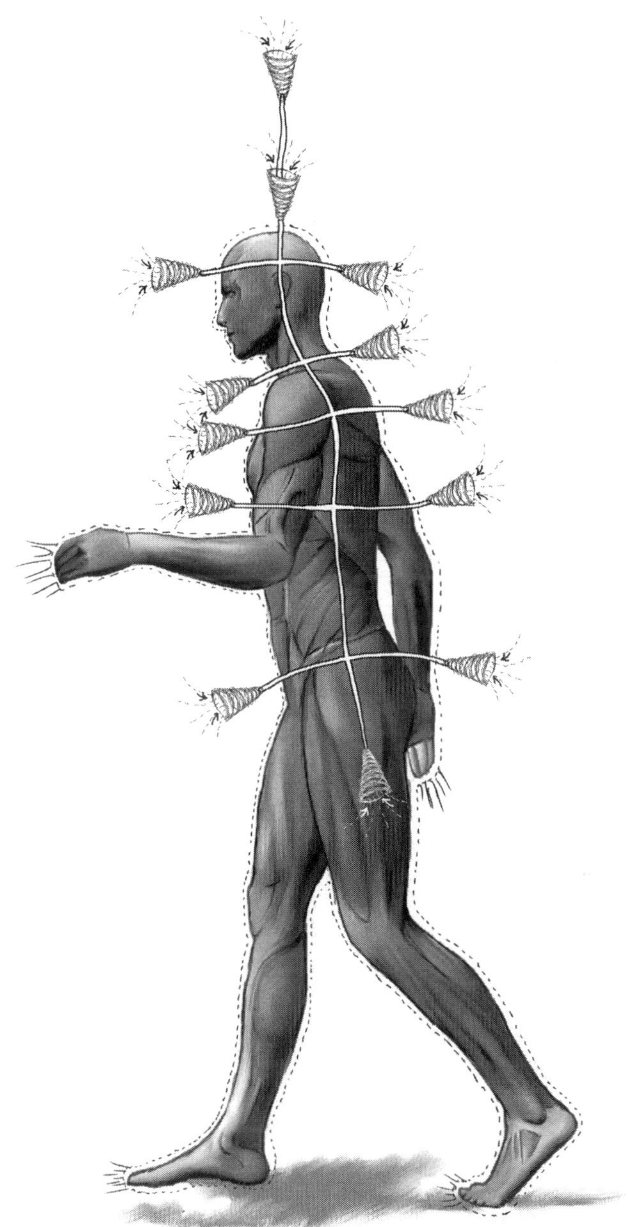

~First or Root Chakra~

The first chakra is located below your spine, connects and grounds you to Mother Earth, and absorbs core energy from the center of the planet. The root chakra stores information about your upbringing and holds the belief systems installed by the village that raised you. Your tribe, family, teachers, friends, and anyone that affected you growing up left thoughts, ideas and formulas for life firmly imprinted in this center to ensure bare survival and adaptation to societal rules.

Imbalance in the first chakra can include problems related to the skeletal system, legs, feet, the elimination system, and loss of the sense of smell.

Typical old energy belief systems in the root chakra are:
"Always consider others first."
"It is not okay to hurt others to be true to your Self."
To replace them with new energy belief systems would sound like this:
"I consider my Self before I consider others to ensure meeting my needs."
"Being true to your Self leads to growth and expansion for all involved."

~

The color associated with the first chakra is red.
The elements connected to the root chakra are metal and earth.
The planet related to the first chakra is Saturn.
The symbol linked to the root chakra is the square.
The musical note the first chakra especially responds to is D.
The sound opening the root chakra is LA.

~

Someone with a balanced root chakra moves forward with ease and grace, has accessible surplus energy safely stored away, includes Self in the bigger picture, is content, grounded, and has created a stable foundation to build upon.

~Second or Abdominal Chakra~

The second chakra is based in the area right underneath the navel and contains information about sexuality, sensuality, and how much you care what other people say or think. It holds your bank account, making sure that you do not overspend your resources. Your lower back could go out if you spend too much of your time, money, support, or give away more manpower than you really can and still take care of your Self.

Here is where you make decisions about basic creations like how many children am I going to have, am I going to rent or buy a house, which car am I going to drive, and what color sweater will I pick.

Imbalance in the abdominal chakra can lead to problems with the reproductive system, kidneys, adrenals, abdomen, lower back, and the loss of the sense of taste or appetite.

Typical old energy belief systems in the second chakra are:
"It is only deserved if it was gained with sweat and blood."
"The more I give and do for others, the more I will get in return."
To replace them with new energy belief systems

would sound like this:
"I aim to create greater results with less effort."
"I include my Self in the bigger picture and take responsibility for my own life."

~

The color associated with the second chakra is orange.
The element connected to the abdominal chakra is water.
The planet related to the second chakra is Jupiter.
The symbol linked to the abdominal chakra is the pyramid.
The musical note the second chakra especially responds to is E.
The sound opening the abdominal chakra is BA.

An individual with a balanced second chakra nurtures the physical body and knows how to fill their basic needs. They regulate the inflow and outflow of resources, make choices based on substance rather than status, create their own formula of happiness, and choose intimate partners that are compatible.

~Third or Solar Plexus Chakra~

The third chakra is situated in the solar or celiac plexus and contains information about inner power, inner wisdom, inner knowing, higher creation and your life's purpose.

Imbalance in the solar plexus chakra can include problems related to the stomach, spleen, pancreas, gall bladder, liver, skin, the muscular system, and the loss of the sense of inner power.

Typical old energy belief systems in the third chakra are:
"Having humility means being humble and that means to be less."
"I am insignificant and small."
To replace them with new energy belief systems would sound like this:
"True humility means that we are all equal -- no one is less, no one is more."
"I am a powerful Light-Being filled with love and light."

~

The color associated with the third chakra is yellow.
The elements connected to the solar plexus chakra are earth and wood.
The planet related to the third chakra is Mars.
The symbol linked to the solar plexus chakra is the circle.
The musical note the third chakra especially responds to is F#.
The sound opening the solar plexus chakra is RA.

~

A person with a balanced third chakra knows the difference between inner power and overpowering others. They are in charge of their life, aware of their true purpose, and living it. They are lined up with their truth and put value on their own inner wisdom and Higher Knowledge.

~Fourth or Heart Chakra~

The fourth chakra is centered in the heart space and contains information about love, joy, compassion, trust, betrayal, hate, grief, and loss. Experience of betrayal or grief closes the heart space and causes isolation and fear. The heart chakra is the most important chakra to be open at this particular time in the evolution of humanity, and the ability to hear the Heart voice is the foundation for decision-making based on integrity.

Imbalance in the fourth chakra can cause complications with the heart, lungs, shoulders, arms, hands, the cardiovascular and circulatory system, the thymus gland, and relates to the loss of sense of touch.

Typical old energy belief systems in the heart chakra are:
"Giving is better than receiving."
"Being selfless is better than being selfish."
To replace them with new energy belief systems would sound like this:
"I receive with open arms and experience the same joy I feel when giving."
"I am true to my Self and joyfully give what overflows from me."

~

The colors associated with the fourth chakra are green and pink.
The elements connected to the heart chakra are fire and metal.
The planet related to the fourth chakra is Venus.
The symbol linked to the heart chakra is the equal arm cross.
The musical notes the fourth chakra especially responds to are A and F.
The sound opening the heart chakra is UM.

~

Someone with a balanced heart chakra has experienced that suffering creates compassion, opened their heart despite the fear of being hurt again, learned that each insult holds a gift, and knows to trust only themselves to know exactly who and what to trust. Loss and grief are viewed as indicators of missing elements within one Self. They use their heart as a gauge for sound decision making, follow their passion, and allow themselves to shower love upon themselves.

~Fifth or Throat Chakra~

The fifth chakra is located at the midpoint of the neck, holds information about communication, and reflects the expression of feelings, emotions, and creations. Holding back or filtering down expression usually results in feeling abandoned and can lead to aggressiveness and violent outbursts. Hearing and listening are important aspects of the throat chakra and range from the ability to truly listen to others to being able to discern between the louder, fear-based Ego voice and the smaller, stiller trust-based Heart voice.

Imbalance in the fifth chakra may include issues related to the jaw, throat, ears, the thyroid gland, and the loss of speech or hearing.
Typical old energy belief systems in the throat chakra are:
"Avoiding conflict creates peace."
"Children should only be seen not heard."
To replace them with new energy belief systems would sound like this:
"I confront conflict in an honest and loving way, staying calm and firm."
"Children are mature Souls in small bodies and deserve equal respect."

~

The color associated with the fifth chakra is aquamarine.
The element connected to the throat chakra is vibrational sound.
The planet related to the fifth chakra is Mercury.
The symbol linked to the throat chakra is the chalice.
The musical note the fifth chakra especially responds to is B.
The sound opening the throat chakra is HA.

~

A person with a balanced throat chakra is congruent with, and aware of, the power of words. They recognize and listen to their true voice and know the difference. Expressing feelings, emotions, and creations in an honest and loving way is second nature. Based on the knowledge that they are interestingly different than others—not wrong or bad—they freely express their own opinions and discern what works for them and what doesn't.

~Sixth or Third Eye Chakra~

The sixth chakra is centered in the area of the third eye, between the eyebrows, and functions like a movie theater. All dreams, ideas and visions are processed in this part of the chakra system. The all-knowing subconscious uses this outlet to send information, pictures, and images to support life's purpose, and inspires new ideas and original concepts or thought forms. The pineal gland at the center of the brain is the literal third eye and functions like a television to gain access to Higher Knowing.

Imbalance in the third eye chakra can include diseases affecting the eyes, the endocrine system, and the pineal gland, and may lead to the loss of the sense of seeing or limited sensory perception.

Typical old energy belief systems in the sixth chakra are:

"It only exists if I can see and measure it."

"Crying is for sissies."

To replace them with new energy belief systems would sound like this:

"I combine science and spirituality to explore all possibilities."

"I show my vulnerability to cleanse my Self and maintain a healthy being."

~

The color associated with the sixth chakra is indigo.

The element connected to the third eye chakra is water.

The celestial body related to the sixth chakra is the Moon.

The symbol linked to the third eye chakra is the Star of David.

The musical note the sixth chakra especially responds to is D.

The sound opening the third eye chakra is AH.

~

An individual with a balanced sixth chakra makes clear choices and decisions, is willing to change their actions until they reach the desired result, and values their ideas, visions, and dreams as important guides. They see opposites as interestingly different rather than right or wrong, and know that sharing their unique viewpoint makes a substantial contribution to the bigger picture.

~Seventh or Crown Chakra~

The seventh chakra spirals upward from the crown of the head and is the direct connection from the physical form to Higher Source, Higher Self, as well as to guards, guides, angels, teachers, and others from the non-physical realm. Closing down the crown chakra leads to feeling separate and abandoned, while being open and tuned in to Higher Source creates flow, ease and an inner knowingness of being One with all that is.

Imbalance in the crown chakra can bring about complications related to the brain, the nervous system, the pituitary gland, and cause the loss of knowledge.

Typical old energy belief systems in the seventh chakra are:

"God is on the outside."

"I am separate and alone."

To replace them with new energy belief systems would sound like this:

"I am Source energy, heavily veiled on the stage of planet Earth."

"I am significant and important in all that is, was, and will be."

~

The color associated with the seventh chakra is violet/crystal.
The element connected to the crown chakra is ether.
The star related to the seventh chakra is the Sun.
The symbol linked to the crown chakra is the lotus.
The musical notes the seventh chakra especially responds to are B and F.
The sound opening the crown chakra is OM.

~

Someone with a balanced crown chakra is connected to Higher Source, recognizes that they are filled with Creator energy, and explores all of their senses, feelings and emotions with enthusiasm and a sense of adventure. They know that they have a solution for each challenge, and trust that everything is in perfect divine order. Treating the Self and everyone and everything that is sentient with reverence and respect is a remarkable trademark of this rewarding way of Being.

~Eighth or Main Central Chakra~

The eighth chakra, which hovers about two or three feet above the head, contains information about, and stores, the Akashic records, which hold the blueprint for each life. It's like a hotel that rents out rooms to archetypes, reflecting all characters and roles needed for the different expressions on the stage of planet Earth. There's the archetype of the Dictator, the Martyr, the Mother, the Victim, the Bully, the Rescuer, the Hero, the Villain, and a whole slew of other personalities and cast members.

Imbalance of the main central chakra may include problems related to clarity, feeling disoriented, repeating patterns, and the loss of the sense of direction.

Typical old energy belief systems in the main central chakra are:
"God could randomly take away my health, wealth or loved ones."
"It's personal when someone hurts me."
To replace them with new energy belief systems would sound like this:
"I grow from and have a solution for everything I put on my plate."
"I remember that we are all playing roles and start looking for the gift."

~

The color associated with the eighth chakra is crystal.
The element connected to the main central chakra is life force energy.
The platform aligned with the eighth chakra is the Universe.
The symbol linked to the main central chakra is the merkahbah.
The musical note the eighth chakra especially responds to is F.
The sound opening the main central chakra is I AM.

A person with a balanced eighth chakra is fully aware that they are playing roles on the stage of life. They recover from feeling like they are a Victim in record time, and realize that they can balance or lay down any role they are immersed in whenever they choose. People with this kind of awareness can transform old patterns gracefully, and, with this, update and rewrite or create a brand new plan for their life's blueprint. This map is stored and kept safe in the library of the Akashic records, which is in constant metamorphosis, and contains all knowledge of human experience and the complete history of the cosmos.

Opus Lux Action Tip

Location is everything! Go directly to the chakra relating to the general area of your physical imbalance and clear the beliefs through an Opus Lux DNAScan made available on www.ChristaRaePacheco.com.

~ Meridians – Pathways of Chi ~

"The doctor of the future will give no medicine, but will interest his patients in the care of the human frame, in diet and in the cause and prevention of disease."
~ Thomas Edison~

Chinese medicine uses the term "jing luo" which means "conduit," "channel," or what has become a familiar term in the western world, "the meridian system." The Incas called the meridians "rios de luz" - rivers of light - and their shamans and healers worked along the same patterns as modern acupuncture, using acupressure and massage to relieve blocks and stagnation.

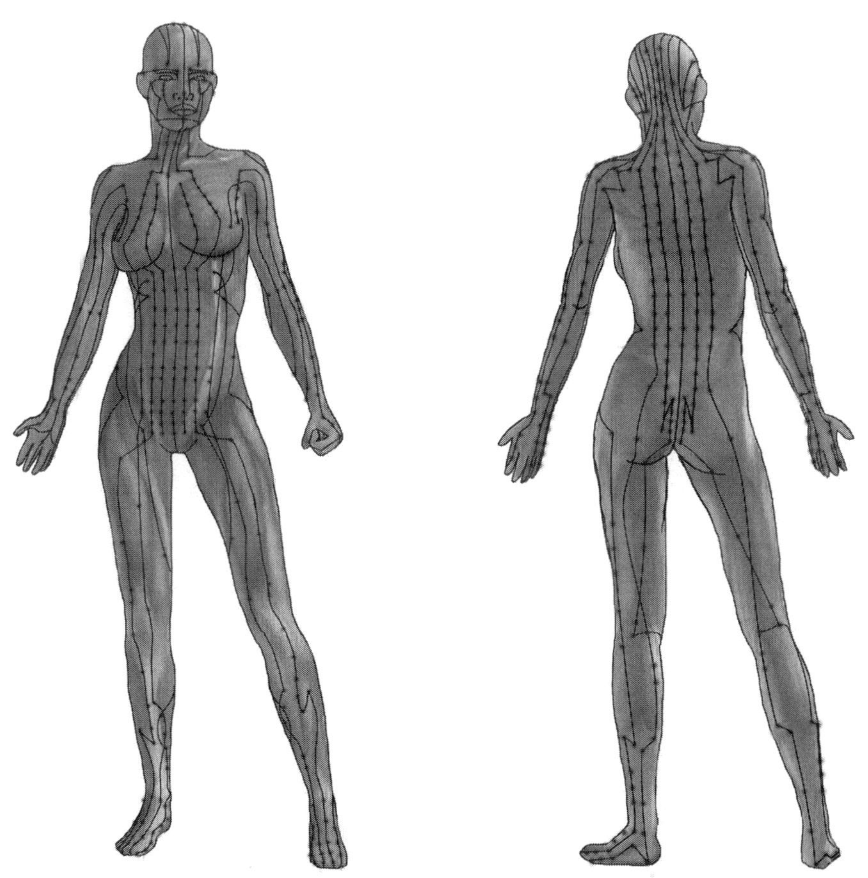

Location of the meridians and acupoints (acupuncture points) in the body.

The meridians are literally rivers that flow through the energy system. For at least 2500 years, Doctors of Acupuncture have used needles to restore flow in the twelve main meridians and eight extra meridians. Each of the twelve main meridians is connected to an organ, and they are mirror reflected on either side of the body. There are always two organ meridians connected. Stomach and spleen, large intestine and lung, gallbladder and liver, bladder and kidney, small intestine and heart, triple energizer and pericardium are paired, and their rivers are linked.

During cell division, the first cell splits into two, separating all Male aspects into what is recognized as the governor vessel and all Female elements into the conception vessel. The governor and conception vessels are connected to all twelve main meridians to strengthen the links between the meridians and regulate the flow of chi and blood circulation.

Imagine that when a tree falls into one of the rivers, it creates a block. The water can no longer flow freely, and the river dries up, creating overflow in the river that is connected. Trees only fall when their foundations are weak, when they have been eroded, or rot away from disease.

~

A skilled Doctor of Acupuncture has knowledge of the exact points and patterns within the over 2000 points used in this ancient method to open and restore the flow of chi. The needles are like tiny antennae, creating a channel for high vibrational life force energy to enter where the low vibrational block or stagnation lies, essentially lifting the metaphorical tree out of the water, so the river can flow in its natural rhythm.

There are roughly 400 acupressure points along the main meridians. Acupressure is applied directly at the site of the blockage. The therapist gently pushes into what feels like an indentation until he feels resistance. Channeling life force energy towards the resistance will soften it and give way to the next tier. An expert will be very patient and sink deeply into the body to release layer after layer until the block is completely removed.

Jin Shin Acutouch simply has the practioner place her fingertips on the far end on either side of the block along the affected meridian. She then feels for a pulse, relaxes, and channels Highest Source life force energy into the meridian being treated until both pulses are in unison, which is the indicator that free flow of chi has been restored.

Reiki, laying on of hands, and massage work with the same principle of channeling Highest Source vibration into the affected area and intentionally raising the lower vibration.

Choose your practioner with care. Remember: The higher the vibration of the healing facilitator, the more profound the effect.

~

So, what exactly causes these blocks? What rots the trees and brings them to fall? And why do the treatments need to be repeated, sometimes for many months, before health has been restored?

Why do countless traditional western medicines just cover up the symptoms and not really heal the imbalance? Medication for depression numbs and suppresses negative emotions and gives the user a false sense of well-being. Being comfortably numb is not a cure. Literally cutting out organs and tissue is common practice and done without much consideration for the overall effect it will have on the patient from a holistic viewpoint. Yes, there is a need for broken bones to be set, injuries to be sewn up, and for medication to be dispensed to temporarily relieve pain.

Many lives have been saved in the operating room, and humanity has greatly benefited from scientifically-designed synthetic medications. Doctors work hard to restore people to health, and, still, something crucial appears to be missing. Is there so much disease to be dealt with that one has to focus on the cure rather than prevention? And is today's western health care built, and leaning heavily, upon a huge money-making profit machine that needs to continue growing to ensure economic and political status?

~

In China, doctors used to be paid to keep their patrons healthy. They listened to the patient's emotional distress and advised with wisdom and care, prescribing exercise, fresh air, rest, a balanced diet, made simple potions with powerful natural herbs, and opened the invisible pathways of chi.

Is the cultivated part of the world becoming more and more prone to disease due to a lack of exercise, being inside all day, and overworked to maintain social standards? Are we eating too many over-processed, chemically- loaded comfort foods, covering up any rebellion from our physical body with designer drugs, and, with that, throwing tree after metaphorical tree into our rivers of light? Have we completely lost touch with the natural flow of our Being? Emotions are stuffed down, polluting us and eating us from the inside out. Smile! No matter what -- pretend that everything is fine. "How are you?" "I'm fine, thank you." Really??

Is it our beliefs, behaviors, perspectives, attitudes and emotions that make us work harder than we need to, stuff our holes with low-vibrational food, vegetate lazy on the couch, or numb the pain of feeling unworthy with a synthetic drug, marijuana or alcohol?

Each cell of your body holds memories of feelings and emotions that were experienced in this or even a past life. The meridians are connected to organs, and each of these organs is a receptacle that holds feelings and emotions. If ignored or stuffed down, emotional garbage breeds disease in the following meridians and their correlating organs, as well as the two containers that separate and hold all Male (Governor Vessel) and all Female energies (Conception Vessel):

Stomach is the home of worry and concern.
Spleen/Pancreas is the home of obsession and frustration over being unable to give more.
Large Intestine is the home of inability to eliminate or release waste or let go of the past.
Lung is the home of inability to live life fully.
Gallbladder is the home of harboring resentment.
Liver is the home of anger and frustration.
Bladder is the home of being "pissed off" and setting the "bar" too high.
Kidney is the home of toxic thought.
Small Intestine is the home of inability to let go of outdated behavior.
Heart is the home of grief and loss.
Triple Energizer (which, in its simplest description, is an organ network of "pipes" that spreads and distributes energy related to the immune and defense system, transports nutrients and body fluids) is the home of excessive using and burning of energy.
Pericardium (which, in its simplest description, is a bagshaped organ which surrounds and protects the organs and vessels of the cardiovascular system) is the home of a lack in what holds joy.
Governor Vessel is the home of imbalance in Male essence.
Conception Vessel is the home of imbalance in Female essence.

~

Imagine for a moment a life in which you know deep in your heart that you have a solution for each challenge and you have all of your needs filled. You have support, negotiate equal exchange, and go with the flow. Personal boundaries are in place and respected, responsibilities are fair, and you are open to new experiences.

You live life fully, are engaged in the creation of your life's mission, and know what love is because you lost it and found it again. Creating greater results with less effort is easy because you make confident decisions and address conflict in an honest and loving way, staying calm and firm.

The Victim role is laid to rest, the "bar" is lowered to a comfortable height, and actions are adjusted until the desired result is actualized. Your formula of happiness is based on what works for you, opinions are freely voiced, your rightful place in the community claimed, and the heart a revered guide.

Feeling safe, important and confident from within is a constant companion. Feelings ranging from being content, to excited, to compassionate, passionate, and enthusiastic is your state of being.

The inner Male works less because he has connected to the inner Female, and this allows for great relationships, a fun-filled, relaxed, synergetic, active life full of abundance, adventure and love.

Sounds nice, doesn't it?

If you knew exactly which belief systems, behaviors, attitudes or perspectives you needed to change to create a life like this, or one of your own specifications, would you be willing to change? Would your metaphorical trees grow stronger, have firmer foundations, and less rot?

~

Why do some people get up from their wheelchairs and walk after drinking the healing water from the sacred healing spring in Lourdes, France, and some are back in it after only two hours? Is it faith or pure luck? What is the difference between someone who gets a chiropractic adjustment where the bone actually stays in place and others who need to go back week after week?

Only those who have changed what causes the imbalance where it originates, deep down at its root, can heal themselves.

The difference is that those who have transformed the negative beliefs that caused the imbalance in the first place need only a simple clearing of the debris in their "river of light" and can easily put things back where they belong on the physical level. Often, a spontaneous physical healing takes place as soon as the negative emotion is transmuted, just like that, no further action needed.

Others hold on to their old beliefs, behaviors and attitudes, and literally mess up the place again and again, in which case it does not matter how skilled or high vibrational the Doctor of Acupuncture, Doctor of Western Medicine, Chiropractic Doctor, or Reiki Master is.

~

The very best healing results are achieved when the negative beliefs, behaviors, attitudes or perspectives about Self, others, and the world in general, are changed to support a positive, empowering view of Self, creating new feelings, responses, and an advanced Higher Consciousness, before any other treatment -- unless there is an immediate crisis at hand.

Once the changes that need to occur have been brought to the surface and active change has begun, depending on the severity and the degree of willingness to change, it will take very few treatments or medications, if any at all, to restore the physical body to perfect health.

The more willing you are to change, the faster you will heal.

Generally people are not consciously aware of exactly which beliefs, behaviors, attitudes, or perspectives actually cause the imbalances in their health, wealth, or relationships. Simply follow these easy steps:

First step to healing:
Give your Self permission to heal, which means that you are willing to change. Download the free e-book "Opus Lux - General Metaphysical Causes," which lists over 700 separate diseases and imbalances or use the Opus Lux DNAScan, both made available on www.ChristaRaePacheco.com to discover and change the individual beliefs, behaviors, attitudes, perspectives, or emotions that caused the imbalance. Then actively change and apply your new beliefs with mindfulness and awareness.

Second step to healing:
Clean up what remains of the fallen trees and clear the meridians with the help of a professional with a high vibration and skill. Acupuncture, Acupressure, Jin Shin Acutouch, Massage, Reiki, or Energy Balancing are some of the options available to help you return to ultimate health and vitality.

Third step to healing:
Yoga, Tai Chi, Pilates, Chi Gong, or gentle physical therapy are excellent ways to open your meridians through movement. Exercise the cardiovascular system with joy and moderation.

Fourth step to healing:
Meditation and visualization of clearing and cleaning away the dead cells to remove the blocks, and replacing them with stem-cell quality, perfect cells, congruent with the original blueprint, is extremely effective. Ask your Higher Guidance to send engineers, technicians, and those best suited from the other realm to help restore and heal your physical body. Envision the body part you are working on return to perfect health. In your mind's eye, see your doctor get really excited about how quickly you have healed, and imagine the positive reaction of your loved ones when they see your progress. Feel the joy and how you will feel when you have returned to perfect health. Express gratitude and appreciation. This exercise only takes a few minutes every day and is extremely productive.

Fifth step to healing:
Your physical body has an inner pharmacy that can produce any

hormone, chemical, nutrient, or painkiller you may need. In a crisis, your body may need help from outside. Replace what your body lost, or is no longer producing, and supplement what it is not getting from food. A Naturopathic Doctor will prescribe natural products that are just as effective, and easier to absorb and tolerate, before writing a prescription for a synthetic drug. A Doctor of Acupuncture has a vast knowledge of the use and benefit of natural herbs and supplements, and considers the effect of the drugs on a holistic level. If you are on synthetic drugs, and would like to get off any prescription drug, ask your Western Medical Doctor to help wean you off in a safe fashion. Never just stop taking prescription drugs. It can have devastating consequences! Your Western Medical Doctor will give you the mildest, most natural product they have in store if you ask for it. Start to replace synthetic drugs with acupuncture and natural herbs. Choose doctors who promote a drug-free life and who are willing to work with you to achieve the best possible treatment for your Highest Good.

Tip: Test your medications, supplements, foods, or anything else, by holding it in your hands while standing up. If your body leans forward, the product will serve you. If your body leans backward, the product is harmful. If your body remains erect, neither leaning forward or back, the product is neutral, which means it will neither serve nor harm you. For some people, leaning back is their positive and leaning forward is their negative. Hold your hands over your heart then say your true name and see which way your body moves, and this is your true positive. Trust your own body. It knows best!

Sixth step to healing:

Eat foods that have been raised and prepared with love, in great variety and in moderation. Get in the habit of testing all foods you eat until you know which products to avoid (see body-dowsing method in above tip). Release food or other allergies with an Opus Lux DNAScan. Drink plenty of high alkaline or pure water.

Seventh step to healing:

Moderation in everything you do and consume creates balance. Stop and smell the roses, rest, sleep in once a week, laugh, play and dance.

Eighth step to healing:

Create a new plan for your life and allow your Self to take the necessary steps. Use the chapter "Living My True Life's Purpose" as a guideline.

Ninth step to healing:
Express gratitude for all that works, all that is good, all you already have, and all you have achieved. Love and embrace where you are today in your life.

~

Barely surviving, neglecting and abandoning Self, low Self-worth, loss of trust, fear of rejection, or a false image of Self, are all misalignments with the authentic Self, and, if ignored, will lead to imbalance in the physical body. Change your perspective, your beliefs, your behavior, your attitude, and it will change how you feel. Changing how you feel will change your reality. You will grow healthy trees with firm foundations and healthy roots. Your rivers of light will thank you for it!

Opus Lux Action Tip
Transform your negative emotions and beliefs about Self and you have taken the most important step in your healing process. After that is done, you will automatically make good choices in all areas of your life, heal at lightning speed, and save thousands of dollars in healthcare.

~DNAScan for your Emotional Body~

"When science begins the study of non-physical phenomena,
it will make more progress in one decade
than in all the previous centuries of existence."
~Nikola Tesla~

Scientific research of the human genome has now proven that if you change your attitude, your perspective, your beliefs or behavior, certain genes turn off while others turn on*.

Imagine that each cell of your body—up to 75 trillion—contain your DNA, two physical and visible chemical strands that are looped and look like a rubber band, and many more invisible-to-the-eye energetic strands. Within the DNA strands are 30,000 protein-based, physically visible genes, plus at least 90,000 invisible-to-the-eye energetic genes, each containing a form of expression.

Physical aspects like hair color, eye color, skin color, bone density, etc., as well as archetypes like the Dictator (Hitler), the Martyr (Mother Teresa), the Lover, the Teacher, the Victim, the Saboteur, the Rescuer, the Villain, are in your genes. You name it, it's a choice. There are emotions, feelings and states of being, patterns, beliefs, and literally anything else that is a form of expression.

Envision each cell as if it was a tiny computer and each gene a program. Some of these programs are turned on to give you an experience on who you are, and some are turned on to give you an experience on who you are not. Some of them are turned off because you do not need them for this particular incarnation. Is it a sign of our society that in American science these genes are known as "junk genes"?

The genetic code of all humans is 99.99% identical, .01% is varied, and no two humans have exactly the same programming.

~

If you loved Louise Hay's book "You Can Heal your Life," you will be surprised and delighted to discover a much larger, extended and vast collection of imbalances covering the characteristics of your physical appearance, diseases of your physical body, organs, systems, psychological imbalances, as well as what causes accidents, spider bites, and much more from a metaphysical standpoint. You will find this new and different collection as a downloadable free e-book with the title "Opus Lux – General Metaphysical Causes" on www.ChristaRaePacheco.com. These evolved insights and examples give you detailed solutions and enhance your ancient knowledge of what your body and Soul are communicating to you. This contemporary, user-friendly list of general metaphysical causes

* Kazuo Murokami, PhD, "The Divine Code of Life."

of imbalance is based on the original Opus Lux – How to Create Your Own Light philosophy.

~

If you are interested in going beyond the general metaphysical causes to explore any of your imbalances from an individual standpoint, or to effectively reprogram your personal DNA, go to www.ChristaRaePacheco.com to book an appointment with a trained healing practitioner using the original Opus Lux DNAScan.

This cutting-edge healing method is designed to literally scan your DNA and reveal the story of which beliefs, behaviors, attitudes, perspectives, emotions or feelings create the imbalances in your health, wealth, career or relationships. Find powerful answers that will heal, balance, and significantly restore your spiritual, mental, emotional and physical bodies, and deliver you to an abundant, meaningful and happy life filled with new possibilities and a wide range of insights about you and your loved ones.

~

How does the Opus Lux DNAScan find which belief creates the behavior that creates the feeling that creates the reality you don't like and would love to change? The answer is very simple:

Your subconscious knows! It is the all-knowing Creator aspect of you, and it will reveal the answers to your quest.

Whenever we are told what we need to change to better our situation, we respond with resistance. It is far more productive to figure it out ourselves by asking our subconscious to give us the answers.

The subconscious knows everything. It knows everything about anything that has ever been, is, and will be. It knows exactly which beliefs, attitudes, perspectives, or behaviors are hidden in your DNA. Your subconscious knows exactly what needs to change to heal your Self and will give you the answers.

The Opus Lux DNAScan process uses a list of written information that contains the common belief systems, behavioral patterns and emotional aspects related to each of the chakras, all meridians, and a great variety of archetypes. Hundreds of emotional aspects, each of the chakras, each of the meridians and a wide variety of archetypes are listed in sections. Within these sections, all related beliefs, behaviors and emotional themes that cause imbalance, as well as the solutions to create balance, are listed and numbered.

Since your subconscious knows everything, it knows the contents and exact information held within each section of the Opus Lux DNAScan list without you ever having to read the information with your physical eyes. The Opus Lux DNAScan is a cutting-edge, contemporary tool to diagnose the core of any imbalance.

The tradition of using objects decorated with symbols or messages to gain insight goes far back in the history of humanity. Ancient Celtic priests kept rune stones in leather pouches. Those seeking advice would reach into the bag, choose a specified number of stones, and the shaman would then interpret the meaning of the symbols to the inquirer.

With the Opus Lux DNAScan process, instead of selecting rune stones, you would be choosing numbers. Each number has a specific meaning, and the different numbers lead to finding which of your beliefs, behavioral patterns, emotions or archetypes are creating the undesirable reality your Soul is begging to change.

Using the subconscious to choose numbers to find the imbalance was inspired by Margaret Ruby, who uses a similar system, and owns and operates the Possibilities DNA Vibrational Healing School in Sagle, ID.

The Opus Lux DNAScan was designed, and is based upon, empirical information gained through many years of facilitating Medical Intuitive services to thousands of clients with a multitude of interestingly different issues, imbalances and diseases. The Opus Lux DNAScan zeroes in like a laser beam and exposes the key components of the beliefs, behavioral patterns and emotions that are the root of disease or imbalance. You are given exact instructions and solutions that are easy to follow, and, when applied, create the desired changes in health, abundance, career or relationships.

To experience the Opus Lux DNAScan, go to www.ChristaRaePacheco.com to find a list of professionally trained, advanced healing practitioners and schedule an appointment. In a typical session, you will discover where the weakest genetic link is, the main theme of your story, which chakra holds the old beliefs, which meridian is impacted, and which archetype needs to be balanced, in order to bring about the desired change. To uproot this information, your healing practitioner will prompt you to choose a number from one to five, one to fourteen, and so forth. Your subconscious knows which numbers to choose and sends an image of the appropriate number to your conscious mind. This is an effortless process which produces impressive results.

You will receive a written transcript of what you are leaving behind, the record of your story of old beliefs, as well as the new beliefs and archetypes that will embrace the changes your Soul desires (see example below).

Change your perspective to change your reality –
heal your Self at the speed with which you are willing to change.

Example transcript using the Opus Lux DNAScan:

Name: Jordan Salazar Age: 18

Release Blurred Vision

Limiting beliefs released:
Genetic trigger: Unrelated person – friend, acquaintance, teacher, etc.
Jordan's best friend shared this pattern and they both pushed each other to the limit.

Main Theme: Fear of rejection.
Jordan remembered that she was not chosen for a sports team in middle school and felt that this must mean that there is something wrong with her.

6th Chakra: Clarity: Distorted view of events.
Jordan felt she had to prove herself by being overly responsible and set her own "bar" extremely high to find the approval and recognition she had lost.

Bladder Meridian: Perfectionism: Fear of disapproval.
Jordan's fear of disapproval led to an exaggerated form of perfectionism.

....

<u>Archetype of Peter Pan:</u>
A childlike or immature wo/man.

Shadow: Careless

1. I am unable to take on adult responsibilities or be accountable, and I depend and rely on others for physical security.
2. I am frustrated with the aging process.
3. I am caught up in being a responsible person, and yearn to feel carefree and light.

Light: Carefree

1. I regain my vitality and power by taking back my own responsibilities. I set my Self free by trusting that I have the ability to take care of my Self and take the necessary steps to support this decision.
2. I have a healthy attitude of remaining young in body, mind, and spirit, enjoying each new phase of life with vitality, playfulness, and curiosity.
3. I regain feeling carefree and light by following my heart and by only taking on what is within my own responsibility.

Essential affirmation: I am carefree and filled with vitality when I follow my heart and only take on what I am truly responsible for.

Jordan felt that number 3 was a true reflection of her pattern. Number 2 was accurate in the sense that she had not allowed her Self to be carefree since losing the spot on the sports team in seventh grade. Number 1 did not apply to her pattern, but it annoyed her when someone displayed these traits, which means that she had gone too far to the opposite side.

....

New perspective:

I now have the clarity to set my own "bar" at a comfortable height, allow my Self to be more carefree, and fill the loss of acceptance and recognition from within.

Jordan wrote a list of all that is great about her, realized that she is not entirely responsible for the success of her current team and needs to allow others to shine as well. She sees more clearly that she had to lose acceptance and recognition before she could become aware of her true talents, abilities, gifts, and how important it is to remain childlike and carefree.

New beliefs:
Transformation of emotions:
Rejection – Approval

I have a choice if being rejected will rob me of my Self-worth or make me stronger, more resilient, and bring me closer to being my authentic Self. I am an expression of highest Source and am interestingly different than everyone else. If I reject anything or anyone that does not fit my personal viewpoint, I may be closing my Self off from interesting new experiences or possibilities. And, it is not important that others accept me. It is important that I accept my Self, exactly as I am.

Essential affirmation: I am accepted when I approve of my Self.

Jordan realized that she was looking for approval from outside her Self and that she would not be accepted exactly the way she is until she learned to approve of her Self.

6th Chakra:

I remember that I am veiled and forgive my Self for falling into the trap of believing that it is outside my own power or doing to change what is happening in my life. I now clearly see that my choices create my reality and observe what I choose with open eyes.

Essential affirmation: I am in charge of my life when I see that my choices create my reality.

Jordan was able to loosen the grip she had on her Self and no longer has to prove her Self. She knows that there is nothing wrong with her if she is not chosen to play in an important game, and understands that her coach may choose others over her for his own reasons and not to hurt her. She has become more of a team player and gets excited when others shine as well.

Bladder Meridian:
I am the only one that can decide what works for me and what doesn't. I am interestingly different than anyone else and allow my Self to live my own purpose. I have a unique task to fulfill and allow my Self to create my own formula of happiness by being true to my Self, setting the "bar" at a comfortable height, and having confidence in my approach. I give the same respect to others and encourage them to follow their own dream.

Essential affirmation: I am my true Self when I set my own "bar" at a comfortable height and create my own formula of happiness.

Jordan has a less competitive attitude and cares more about having fun. This allows her to confirm her strengths, yet remain carefree and light.

Opus Lux Action Tip
The Ego does not like change and may throw a major tantrum when you introduce the idea of new ways of doing or being. Just by recognizing and ignoring this interference, you are 50% closer to healing.

~ 2012 – End Times? ~

"It had literally been the darkest hour before the dawn."
~Martin Luther King~

2012 -- End Times? Yes, absolutely, but only the end of bad times, and the beginning of a new world of equanimity, abundance, and love.

~

More people have been asking what to expect as we approach 2012. They have come across many scary stories online, in books, movies, and in the news. Most of these sources are steeped in the Old Order and interpret the Bible, Nostradamus' writings or the ending of the Mayan calendar for Self-serving purposes and to spread fear. The old energy stamp was, after all, "Fear will create control, and control will create a sense of outer power."

Instead of being scared, could we be excited about these so-called End Times?

We are at the end of a dark cycle and at the beginning of a time where we will live as enlightened Beings in a world of harmony, balance, and abundance. A willingness to change the perspectives, attitudes, beliefs, and behaviors that cause undesirable results is the first step to this long-awaited way of living. The vibration on planet Earth is rising, and change is coming easier and faster than at any time before. A new day is dawning!

~

Everything on the plane of Mother Earth is cyclical and is designed for the experience of duality. Day follows night, dry is replaced by wet, hot turns into cold, and suffering exists to create compassion and the ability to truly understand what compassion is.

For thousands of years humanity has been in a dark cycle, heavily veiled to experience mainly who we are not. We came here to either create suffering or to endure suffering. We battled wars and were afflicted by disease. We plundered the Earth and saw limitation and scarcity everywhere we looked. We became greedy or Self-less, powerless or dictatorial beings, here to destroy and to learn how not to be.

Humanity has gone through this before and has always destroyed itself at the end of a dark cycle, gone back to the non-physical realm, and returned newly programmed and equipped to be able to enter into the new light cycle. This is the first time in human history on the planet Earth in which we are evolved enough to stay and move from a dark cycle into a light cycle without having to die.

On August 16 and 17, 1987, we had a planetary alignment we called "The Harmonic Convergence" which indicated the imminent approach of a new cycle. As this grand trine occurred, the collective consciousness of humanity was asked on a subconscious level if we were ready to stay, instead of destroying ourselves like we have done at the end of dark cycles in previous times. We will get to release our old programming, shed the beliefs that support being mainly who we are not, clean up the mess, and move into a new light cycle to live abundant, fulfilling lives, and be mostly who we truly are.

Instead of destroying our well-being, we will create health, wealth, and treat the environment and everyone in it, including ourselves, with respect and honor. The old energy stamp of "Fear will create control, and control will create a sense of outer power," will be replaced with the new energy stamp of "Trusting Self will lead to healthy decisions, and making heart-based choices will lead to standing in the power of who we truly are." On a collective subconscious level, humanity said "Yes!" and started to clean up the mess.

~

Imagine that we are at a point where the dark and the light cycles are slightly overlapping, creating a space in between that is neither black nor white. It is a lot like experiencing the dawning of a new day, and it got underway literally with what appeared to be the darkest hour before dawn. The dragons started to raise their heads one last time in an attempt for survival of greed, disease, war and corruption.

People started to question their abusive or status-oriented relationships and left. They filed for bankruptcy over their blown-out-of-control credit cards, were forced to create budgets and live within their true means. Some could no longer pay the mortgages on the houses that were more expensive than they could actually afford, were forced to pack up and move into housing within their means. Many lost their corporate or otherwise stifling jobs and were called to discover their true passion and life's mission. Mothers began standing up to end the senseless killing of their sons and daughters in wars based on lies, solely designed to bring about economic benefits, and, to the astonishment of those in control, started awareness campaigns to show us that the only one that wins is death.

~

We are at the gateway now. Looking back before we step through to the other side, these questions arise: Have we learned enough about how not to be? Are we ready to take our power back and move into being who we truly are? Can we take on the challenge of cleansing ourselves of everything that no longer serves us and change into being the powerful Creators we really are?

~

It is dawn now. We can finally see, after being in the dark
for a long time.

By 2012 it will be day.
Everything will be brilliantly visible to the naked eye.

With the veils of darkness removed, the majority of humanity will discover that they are immortal. The realization that the energy which animates all sentient physical forms that exist on Mother Earth cannot be killed and lives on outside of physical form is mind-blowing for many and is a new concept supported by today's science. Energy can change form, but it cannot be annihilated or converted to be non-existent—even when it becomes invisible to the naked eye.

You may ask, "What makes a sentient Being sentient?" and the answer is, "Source energy." Our Souls, slivers of all-encompassing Source energy, can come and go as they please—again and again.

~

Once we recognize our divinity, we will treat ourselves and all other sentient Beings with reverence and respect. A true understanding of equality will allow us to celebrate our differences and prompt us to be mindful of all of creation. The insight that we are perfect as a whole, each of us individually holding an important piece of all that is, will restore our knowledge that we create the most desirable outcomes by honoring each other. Each and every one of us is important in the bigger picture and matters greatly in the creation of the new world.

~

Our physical bodies are designed to live much longer than we currently anticipate. When disease is a memory of the past, when the physical body is fed with high-vibrational food, pure water, clean air, when it gets enough rest, receives loving touch and moderate exercise, the human vehicle will thrive.

Right now, most of us treat our automobiles better than the sacred vehicle of our Souls. Imagine that your physical body is a high-end luxury car and act accordingly!

Does being immortal mean that we will indefinitely stay in our present-time physical body? Would you have a desire to drive the same car with the same technology and the same need for a specific fuel for the "remainder" of eternity? Probably not. Evolving from one form into another, choosing anew something that is interestingly different, allows Source to experience itself in all possible ways. Driving a well-cared-for high-end vehicle is more fun than driving a cheap, abused and neglected wreck. Polish your physical body. Give it what it needs so that your immortal Soul can have a long, deliciously rewarding stay before it has to start looking for a new vehicle.

Time in and of itself is a necessary deception to support the illusion of a beginning, middle, and an end. Past, present, future; being born an innocent babe, growing from life experiences, and finally dying as an old, wise sage, is how we experience cycles, and the entire range of emotions and feelings show us who we are not and who we truly are. Day and night, spring and fall, summer and winter, ebb and flow, poverty and prosperity, being heavily veiled and attaining enlightenment, all are designed so we can experience opposites, duality, and all possible ways of being.

It is our linear thinking, the way things look to us, and how we interpret our very own nervous system that makes it seem that time flows. The fact is, time does not pass. We pass. Our linear thinking demands to know where we are right now. We need order to stay sane on the stage of Earth.

In simple Earth terms, we are at the very beginning of creating lives filled with happiness, joy, fulfillment, abundance, loving relationships, financially and creatively rewarding careers, dynamic health, sustainable economy, spiritual enlightenment, and any other desired experience that we can imagine.

We leave behind us a trying cycle of suffering, disease, wars and ignorance. By the time the new cycle of light has completed, our Souls will be excited to don the heavy veils once again, draw the curtains, and succumb to another cycle of darkness. Night follows day and day follows night. Celebrate, even if you are bloody and tired after the battle. Restore, redress, renew.

~

Remember that your choices and decisions create your reality; that you hold the steering wheel firmly in your own hands and are decidedly in control of how you respond to what you attract to your Self.

Opus Lux Action Tip

Focus on your Self until you have created balance in your own life, and until you overflow, before helping others.

~ Old vs. New Human Energy ~

"In order to change, we must be sick and tired of being sick and tired."
~Author Unknown~

Every child born since 2000, and many that came in before, even a handful as far back as the '50s, is programmed for the new light cycle. They have been called "Indigo Children," "Crystalline Children," "Star Kids," "Angels on Earth," "Old Souls," and an array of other equally compelling names. As a whole, they represent the new humanity.

New humans are here to experience harmony, balance, and peace. They are here to create, not to destroy. Lesser veils allow them to innately, and on a very deep level, know that they are supreme Light-Beings having a physical experience on the stage of Earth.

Imagine the shock many of them experienced when they were exposed to the harsh reality created by the previous energy humans who were born with the old energy stamp of the now-ending dark cycle. These newly programmed children had to endure being treated with disrespect, were faced with huge mountains of garbage of all kinds, a world that fights each other, fights disease, focuses on everything it dislikes, and has brought misery not just to their own kind, but inflicted pain on all sentient Beings, including Mother Earth. So much to fix, so much to overcome, so much to change!

They feel overwhelmed with having to deal with their previous energy parents, relatives, teachers, bosses, school systems, governments, a negative entertainment industry, and even friends, whose perspectives, attitudes, behaviors and beliefs distort the original blueprint of these beautiful new humans. All of the above contributes to what drives some of them to use drugs, while others act out with violence, become insecure, feel isolated, or respond with depression.

Typically a new human feels crushed by the amount of change that needs to take place in order to create the life they came here to experience. Great relief usually washes over them when they discover that there is no need to take down the old in order to build the new. What you ignore wastes away. What you focus on grows. Once they realize that they are here to create, not to destroy, and that all they need to do is take a good look at the old to know what creates the existing imbalance, off they go with focus on what needs to be put into place to create solutions and answers that will clarify and actualize desirable results.

~

What is going to happen with the people who were born into the previous energy? Are they doomed to stay the way they are, or is there something they can do to change their old programming?

Envision for a moment the excitement of having been born into the limitations and constrictions of coming into physical form to mostly be who we are not, and then, for the first time in human history on planet Earth, to move into a light cycle and shed all beliefs, behaviors, attitudes, and perspectives that are no longer congruent with the new, to come up with an updated plan, and transform into becoming a new human. It's a lot like a caterpillar deciding to turn itself into a butterfly. What an adventure!

Being heavily veiled doesn't support this metamorphosis, nor does feeling the pressure of having to change. Change appears to be the biggest threat to the Ego and is one of the most challenging feats to accomplish. Humans are creatures of habit. We thrive on routines and patterns. Practicing the same routine and pattern helps us to sharpen our skills. The difference between a rookie driver and an experienced one is due to practicing the same routines over and over. If you learned to play tennis on your own, and then took lessons with a pro, you would have to spend a lot of time just erasing ineffective skills. What we routinely practice becomes a deeply ingrained habit. We proudly announce that we haven't changed at all, and defend even the worst of traits with comments like, "That's just who I am, take it or leave it."

Every one of the old guard still on the planet at this point in history expressed a desire to shed their obsolete, old skins, and step into the contemporary, sleek, comfortable clothing of the new cycle. Those who cannot change, despite their willingness, will return back to the light. Sometimes it's easier to come up with a brand new plan, step into a new human body, and return to the plane of duality with a program designed for the new cycle. This could explain the greater number of seemingly unnecessary or sudden deaths in the last few years, and leading up to 2012.

~

Learning to understand the differences is the first step. A willingness to change and recognize the need to support one another is a close runner-up. Once we understand why someone does what they do, we can accept. And once we accept, we can unconditionally love.

Here is a short list of conventional previous human attitudes:

I know better because I'm older.
I can control situations with force.
I believe only what I see.
I am worth less because I am a woman, have dark skin, am poor, etc.
I get to rule because I am a man, your father, your husband, your boss.
I believe in a God outside myself and fear judgment.

I rely solely on logic, and hard work will get me to my goals.
I focus on all I dislike, everything that angers, irritates, or frustrates me.
I am the way I am and cannot change.
I only care that something is cheap, not how it has come into existence.
I fight against terrorism, breast cancer, poverty, etc.
I say things I don't really mean to get others off my back.

And here is a general list of new human attitudes:

I can foresee the consequences of my actions, even at an early age.
I guide others, share information, and communicate to manage any situation.
I connect to my Higher Knowing to explore all possibilities.
I am equally important and matter just as much as everyone else.
I can only be a good leader when I respect others as much as my Self.
I trust my Higher Self and treat my Self and all other sentient Beings with reverence and respect.
I create greater results with less effort by combining my heart and mind.
I focus on what works, what I already have, and what I would like to create.
I am constantly growing and evolving.
I reduce my carbon footprint by buying higher quality products that last longer and have been created with love, care, and mindfulness.
I find ways to create more peace and live as an example by filling my own needs first and by only giving away what overflows from me.
I am congruent with my words and actions, even if this proves to be inconvenient for others.

~

Be the proverbial light tower and lead the way by living the way you would like others to live. The minute you have created a life for your Self that is filled with harmonious relationships, vibrant health, a lucrative and fulfilling occupation, intellectual and spiritual stimulation, and lots of fun, play, and laughter, everyone else is going to beg you for the recipe! It's not so much in preaching these changes. It's in actually living them. Unless you live what you teach, no one is going to believe you.

Previous energy human, are you willing to change and become the new? New human, are you willing to understand why your dad, mom, or boss, is acting according to their ingrained belief systems based on an old paradigm? They are not causing you pain because they don't love you or because there is something wrong with you! You are just interestingly different and in the process of a major transformation. Moving from a dark cycle into a light cycle while staying in our physical bodies has not been done before. It's a first in human history on planet Earth, and it is the single most exciting event humanity has ever experienced. Patience, guidance, information, and communication are essential to bridging the gap and creating a new way of life.

~

The new children are not just in tune with their exceptional extrasensory perception, seemingly wiser due to having lesser veils, and know who they truly are; they are typically also programmed to be highly manipulative. They will manipulate you relentlessly until you finally respect your Self, set personal boundaries, and learn to confidently stand in your own power. That's their job! They love to be guided, informed, and shown by good example, and will respond to control and injustice with outrage.

ADD, ADHD, Autism, and Asperger Syndrome are all terms we have become familiar with. For the first time in recorded history, Souls are incarnating into physical form with a much higher vibration than ever before. Our physical body is used to a lower vibration, and the Souls that are having trouble holding a higher vibration while staying in the physical form are those we label with the above terms.

There is no cellular memory of how a Soul can stay in a physical body with this high of a vibration. We need to help those who have a hard time anchoring into their physical bodies by creating the best possible environment for them. The inability to successfully join the physical body with the new higher-vibrational Soul energy signifies a need for change. You will observe the phenomena of Autism and its cousins slowly disappear over the next ten to twenty years. People will learn to stay in their physical bodies while holding a much higher vibration and this creates cell memory for future generations.

The question of whether childhood disease prevention vaccines can cause Autism is dependent on how well your high-vibrational child can stay in his physical body when injected with a dose of low-vibrational virus-infested solution. Especially MMR (measles, mumps and rubella) is dangerous for some children. A triple dose of very old, extremely low-vibrational virus strands may be too much all at one time.

Always test all medication, vaccines, supplements, foods, or anything else by holding it in your hands while standing up. If your body leans forward, the product will serve you or the person you are asking for (like your child). If your body leans backwards, the product is harmful. If your body remains erect, neither leaning forward nor back, the product is neutral, which means it will neither serve nor harm you. For some people leaning back is their positive and leaning forward is their negative. Place your hands on your heart, say your true name, see which way your body moves, and this is your true positive. Trust your own body. It knows best. It is perfectly fine to test your child's medication or vaccine in your doctor's office. Teach this body dowsing method to your child as soon as possible. It will help your child to make lifestyle choices that serve his or her individual and personal needs.

Ask your pediatrician if the MMR vaccine can be administered in separate doses, and only when your child tests positive. A different brand, waiting until the child has reached a more mature age, or an energetic microbial balancing treatment accompanying the immunization procedure can make a huge difference. If your child already has a cold or is tired, schedule a new appointment time for the vaccination.

In the meantime, the new humanity is no longer going to focus on negativity, or learn anything irrelevant to their individual purpose. They are no longer willing to be controlled and disrespected, and are tired of ingesting pesticides, abused foods, and synthetic drugs designed to curb their sense of carefreeness and personal freedom.

These new children will let you know when something is glaringly out of balance. Hysterical outbursts, disproportionate back-talking, being disrespectful, disrupting conversations, screaming, howling, trashing things, indifference, or severe withdrawal are just a few items on the list of how they try to get your attention. You will know. Please pay attention! Communicate, make changes, and truly listen. Stop turning them into walking zombies by poisoning them with medications designed to quiet them down or engineered to bring them out of their protective shells.

Give them what their Souls are begging for. Ease their pain by giving attention to all that is positive. Praise them for all their good qualities and every time they do something that creates the desired result. Reward them instead of taking privileges away. Just like you, they are more motivated to do chores when they know exactly what is expected and when they can earn their allowance, a special outing, internet access, or computer time.

Get involved. As a family, come up with house rules, chore charts, and consequences that are age appropriate. These rules need to be upheld by all involved, including you. You cannot seriously expect your child to use clean language, stay away from harmful substances, or demonstrate follow-through, if you don't. As you sit together to create these rules and intentions for living together in harmony, listen to and consider all objections, ideas, and preferences until a plan emerges with which everyone is in agreement.

Make school an interesting and fun environment to explore and grow in. Consider home schooling, private schools like Montessori or Waldorf, or be an active participant in your child's public school experience. Treat them with the respect you would normally reserve for the most admired, most revered person in your life.

Feed them foods that have been raised and prepared with love. Look at your own diet and level of fitness. If you make poor lifestyle choices, you are more likely to allow your children to choose highly-processed foods, as well. You may not realize that they are malnourished and their little bodies are wasting away from inactivity. How can a human thrive on packaged Ramen noodles, candy-bars, potato-chips and soda?

The consequences can be devastating. These new Beings are not invincible. The rising incidences of diabetes, obesity and severe underweight observed in today's children, is closely related to lazy and overindulgent lifestyle choices. Remember that any extreme will lead to imbalance. If you are pushing them too hard, are too strict, or exercise them as if you were running a boot-camp, stop and consider a more moderate approach.

An inscription over the temple entrance in Delphi, Greece, states "Know Thyself" and "Nothing in Excess," which invites you to know your Self and those you are responsible for so well that you would be aware of what constitutes moderation.

Turn off the TV, computer, or video games more often, and give them the gift of quality time and loving attention. Play with them. Get to know them.

Make sure they play with other kids, get plenty of fresh air, sunshine, and participate in physical activities that are fun. Isolating them will lead to anti-social behavior and loneliness. Engage them in conversation and be amazed at the wisdom coming out of even the youngest representative of the new humanity.

New humans love being given choices. For example, if you have a three- year-old who greatly resists his bedtime because he doesn't like being controlled, simply offer him a choice and he will respond beautifully and feel in charge of his own life. Ask if he would like to wear this pajama or that, to listen to a story or sing a lullaby. Two choices are usually enough to eliminate the power struggle between child and guardian.

Once you understand the differences and why they exist, you can accept, understand, and unconditionally love and support one another.

The new world needs a new order, new systems, new paradigms, and new ways of dealing with duality. We are on the verge of creating synergy by combining science and spirit, old and new, mind and heart. Who but you is going to look at the bigger picture with clarity and foresight? We have a choice. We can help one another, cheer each other on, forgive each other for the mistakes that were made in the past, act like we actually know deep within our Souls that this is the turning point, and realize that we are the ones we have been waiting for.

Opus Lux Action Tip

Look around and discern which of the people you know were born into the previous energy and which decided to come in fully equipped for the new. This will help you to understand and support them from a different viewpoint.

~Living My True Life's Purpose~

"Start by doing what's necessary, then do what is possible, and suddenly you are doing the impossible."
~St. Francis of Assisi~

Living your life's true purpose is essential to feeling happy, healthy, and whole. Each and every one of us has a calling, a life's mission, and is fully equipped with the exact amount of intelligence, the perfect talents, strengths, abilities, and gifts to live it to its fullest potential. All knowledge gained, all tasks mastered, and all experiences had, add to, and are part of, your true life's purpose. There are no wasted moments, no job done, that didn't somehow serve in the fulfillment of the bigger picture, and no wrong place to have been at any given time.

If everyone did what they came here to do, everything would be done.

Some people know exactly what their calling is at an early age and head steadfast into the direction of their dreams. Others are never quite sure, or just take what life hands them, without much aim or any particular plan. Few truly do for a living what they are passionate about and most wouldn't dare to dream that they could possibly be successful by being who they are, doing what they love.

Patriarchy has taught that only those who rely on their left brain logic, those determined to work hard in a world of competition, those who can muster up the courage to undergo tests of endurance, and those who possess a willingness to sell out, are going to "make it." The use of intuition, creativity, or making choices based on how something feels was deemed worthless in this Male-dominated world. Fostering fear created being in control, and being in control meant having a sense of outer power. Those who had outer power ruled and all others bowed down.

~

Being successful in the new world allows for the distribution of wealth to all who desire it and inspires creating greater results with less effort. "Ease" and "grace" are key words. And instead of being in the Archetype of the Magician, who works hard to create an illusion of success, more and more emphasis is put on becoming a Wizard. The Wizard's secret is to use the feminine aspects of inner knowing, application of inner wisdom, listening to the Heart voice, and choosing what feels exciting, first, and then combining them with the Male aspects of planning, logic, and action, to create synergistic desirable outcomes with minimal challenge and very little effort.

The key to success is being and doing what you are passionate about. One way to find your passion is to write down a short version of your autobiography. Look at what you were lacking in your life, what was important, and what ignited your passion.

Another way is to write down on note cards all that you love to do and be. Write down everything you can think of: Dancing, sleeping, camping, reading, giving massages, kids, favorite places, cooking, analyzing, working as a team, being a leader, organizing, planning, your spirituality, care-giving, flowers, being a peacemaker, or anything else that you can possibly come up with. Then sort the cards by priority, what is more important, this or that, until you have just three or four cards left. These are your power cards and they're great indicators of your deepest passions. Combined they can show you what you are here to do.

Examples:

Writing poetry, working from home, sharing wisdom -- a greeting card manufacturer may be waiting just for you!

Problem solving, intellectual stimulation, science -- are you an Inventor?

Kids, parenting, crafting -- could you give workshops or create an e-book or video on crafting for parents who realize how important it is to spend creative time with their kids and need some ideas?

Environment, teamwork, creating solutions -- companies with a conscience are always looking for consultants with green concepts.

Fashion, shopping, passion for helping others -- you could offer a service that helps those who desire to look great but don't know how.

Dogs, hiking, traveling -- how about a career as a Truffle Hunter?

~

No matter how insignificant your contribution to the world may look from the Ego's standpoint, every single purpose, each life's calling, is an important mission. Without the janitor, the president would be in brown stuff up to his or her ears. If we were all Einstein's, who would grow our foods, teach our children, build our houses, or write a delightful play that's going to make us laugh and forget the "real world" for a moment?

~

Create your own Living My True Life's Purpose plan.

Put your plan in writing. Actually writing something down gives it more power and brings it into a denser, more physical form. Use your imagination, and, if necessary, pretend that you are on a neutral slate, free of responsibilities or obligations.

Imagine that you only have five years to live, are in perfect health, and that you have access to any and all resources that you could possibly ever need for whatever you plan to do or be. Resources are time, money, support, manpower, technology, and anything else you might need for your creation.

You have already traveled the world and are fully rested. What would you create within those five years if you would like to leave something behind of your Self from which others can benefit? This can be an idea, a book, an empire, or a service -- anything from very simple to highly complex.

~

Look around and see if you can find people that you admire and respect because of what they stand for, how they live, who they are, what they've created, or what is important to them. These are indications showing you valuable components of who you are and would like to become more of. Integrate their traits, copy what you like, and always be sure to make the trait your own version, adapting it to fit your own mission and personality. With this exercise, you are simply expanding on who you already recognize you are.

Your Ego voice might tell you that somebody already did what you are about to do. Your Heart voice will remind you that it is very rare to be the very first to come up with a brand new idea or concept, and that even though you may be using ancient knowledge and existing elements, information or concepts, you must trust that you will put the pieces together like no one ever has before; thus, using the power of alchemy to cause evolution and to manifest something that has never been.

~

Envision the highest goal you can imagine for your Self and write down all the steps that you can think of to get you there. On different sheets of paper write down at least five of the smaller goals you need to reach to achieve your main goal. On each of these goals write down all the steps you can imagine it will take to accomplish, and then start taking the first steps toward your goals. You will meet the right people, and doors will open as you move forward.

~

Write down how you would like to live – where, what kind of house, with whom you would live, what your optimal day would look like, how you would spend your time, what you might do and create if you had no fear and completely trusted that you always had everything you could possibly ever need for whatever you planned.

~

Take action and do what is possible each day. You will notice that you always have exactly what you need on that particular day. Waiting around for an investor, a better time, or until greater knowledge has been acquired only wastes time. There is always something that can be done in the meantime – meaning now -- that will get you closer to the highest vision of your Self.

The realization that you cannot unfold the pedals of a rosebud without tearing it gives you the patience to let each step that's needed gracefully reveal itself. Become comfortable with mystery. You cannot know exactly how everything will fall into place. Intend that what you have chosen will come to you with ease and grace and for the Highest Good of all involved. Then if something does not go how you had envisioned, know that something better is waiting, usually right around the corner. Your Higher Self will have a different solution ready for you, most likely one you are just not aware of yet. Divine timing could play a role in the perceived delay. Keep polishing, be patient, and learn from those who have already accomplished similar goals.

In the interim, be grateful for what you already have, celebrate each accomplishment no matter how small, and trust that what you would like to draw into your life is on its way.

~

Instead of having to prove to others or your Self that you can reach your highest vision of your Self, make it an experiment to see how close you can get to the highest vision of your Self. Making it an experiment takes off the pressure and allows for "failures" and "mistakes," which are our greatest teachers. It gives you permission to start over, and eliminates the inclination to give up when challenges arise.

~

Remember to make decisions based on the joy and enthusiasm you feel in your heart before using your logic to plan.

Look at your past to decide what you did not like,
choose for your future what you
would have liked to have had in your past,
then take action and modify your behavior in the NOW to create it.

Close your eyes for a moment and use your extrasensory vision to look out over the ocean. If you had a ship and a captain, could you go to the place where the sky meets the water? You could, but by the time you would get to the spot where the sky met the water when you were standing on the shore, it would have shifted, the horizon again far in the distance. It is the same with your goals. By the time you have reached the highest vision of what you can imagine now your goals will have expanded to an even greater vision. You could end up chasing the horizon in a never-ending race, get exhausted, and lose the passion and enthusiasm that once ignited the fire. Make sure to be aware that your highest vision constantly evolves to the next highest version, and remind your Self to take the time to celebrate each accomplishment along the way, each destination reached, each task fulfilled, and each glorious moment experienced that got you closer to being who you are, doing what you love.

 ***Opus Lux Action Tip***

It only takes about twenty minutes to come up with a rough draft of your own "Living My True Life's Purpose" plan. Why delay? Do it now! You are free to make changes along the way, polish, enhance, add to, or write a brand-new version whenever you feel like it! In fact, it's a good idea to review and revamp your plan every few months.

~ Inner Male meets Inner Female ~

"The intuitive mind is a sacred gift
and the rational mind is a faithful servant.
We have created a society that honors the servant
and has forgotten the gift."
~Albert Einstein~

Chinese Medicine teaches that when the first cell splits in two, one holds all feminine qualities and the other holds all male qualities. On a very fundamental level, the world of duality requires such separation and has highlighted both Matriarchy and Patriarchy as the only possible consequence created by this disconnection.

The era of ancient Matriarchy is widely disputed, and its only evidence appears to be an overwhelming amount of archeological finds, many that date from the Neolithic period in the New Stone Age in ancient Egypt and other early historical cultures. The discovery of Mother Goddess statues, voluptuous female icons, and a variety of prehistoric images, shows that many ancient cultures worshiped female deities, and indirectly tells the story of admiration and honor for the feminine qualities.

A society headed by the female gender and based on feminine characteristics such as listening to inner knowing, following inner wisdom, nurturing, creativity and passive conflict resolution is, after all, hard to imagine, and raises many questions within the Male-dominated society of the 21st century.

With the onset of structured agriculture and advances of scientific accomplishments, logic, reason, and a growing interest in ownership and competition soon overruled the ideals of the feminine standard and resulted in supremacy of Patriarchy. Intuition, creativity, and the attributes of softness, compassion, rest, and play were judged to be worthless and were ridiculed. Anyone who openly used their intuition, psychic abilities, or extrasensory perception was eliminated, killed, silenced, dismissed, or incarcerated.

~

Having had a history of both Matriarchy and Patriarchy, we are well aware of the qualities as well as the limitations inherent in each and have arrived at a crossroads once again.

In the new way of living, will the Feminine rise to extinguish and smother the bright flame of the Male rule, or will the physically stronger men stay in command? What does it mean when the return of the Goddess, the return of the Feminine rule, is prophesized, announced, and glaringly imminent?

~

No matter what gender you were born into, you were most likely taught that using the Male qualities of logic, reasoning and hard work will assure monetary success, which promises you the ability to survive in a harsh environment, and to give you a sense of accomplishment and social esteem. It is no surprise that these Male-oriented formulas simply dismiss the notion of using inner power, inner wisdom, and extrasensory perception as guiding tools.

No matter what gender you were born into, you have an inner Male and an inner Female. The inner Male has worked hard, has bravely fought many battles, and at this time in history is tired, bloody, and exhausted. The inner Female, in the meantime, has retreated and held back. She has become submissive, feels worthless, and has lost trust in her abilities.

Close your eyes for a moment and look at your own inner Male and your own inner Female. If they were people, what would they look like? Is your inner Male gigantic, muscular and overpowering next to your inner Female? Is he ignorant of her strengths, dismissing her gifts, talents, and abilities, or has her dependency and passiveness taken over, leaving him drained and weak? Take some time to examine their relationship. Do they know each other? Do they respect each other's qualities? Do they work together, talk to each other, support each other, and believe in creating synergy to create greater results with less effort?

When the qualities of both the inner Female and the inner Male are combined, the synergy creates greater results with less effort.

As we stand at the crossroads, we are invited to choose both, to integrate the amazing qualities of both the Male and Female aspects, and invent a new way of living. By creating a connection between the inner Female and the inner Male, a connection between heart and mind is established. When you combine forces, synergy is created. One horse pulls one ton, two horses pull four tons. Imagine the potential of connecting science and spirituality, logic and intuition, thinking and feeling. It is no longer one or the other. It is about seeing the greatness in both qualities and combining them for ultimate harmony. Ask your Self if it is really true that we have evolved to this point in history by eliminating the weaker and smaller or by cooperation and collaboration. If all the energy used to destroy spirituality, intuition, and feelings were channeled into figuring out how to combine them with science, logic, and thinking, the resulting possibilities would produce unlimited and vastly accelerated effects.

~

Our outer relationships reflect our inner relationship between the inner Female and the inner Male. Pay close attention to who is boss, which one plays the role of being submissive, and how this perfectly reflects what goes on inside of you. Have you stepped into the Male role so much that your femininity is covered up by power suits or by hiding under your husband's oversized flannel shirts? Have you been emasculated by women who do everything they can to steal your power because they have lost theirs and that's the only way they know how to feel powerful and in control of their lives? The variety of imbalances is countless and, interestingly enough is always reflected by our outer relationships.

Look at President Obama. His inner Male and his inner Female are perfectly balanced. His outer relationship with his wife, Michelle, indicates a union between two whole beings that celebrate each other's qualities and demonstrate equality and respect. He has and will make decisions that are based on equal energy between his inner Female and his inner Male -- which is interestingly different. He is obviously breaking the rules of Patriarchy, which leads to scrutiny and provokes unified head shaking from those still programmed to the old ways of ruling a country or kingdom.

~

Talking about kingdoms and equality, a few years ago our British neighbors across the Atlantic Ocean presented us with a real life drama designed to announce the decay of Patriarchy and put a stop to seeing our traditional role plays as desirable. Most of us remember the day when the news announced that Princess Diana had died in a tragic car accident, speeding through a tunnel to escape the pursuing paparazzi.

A wave of sympathy and great loss swept through a large part of the world. Women especially mourned and felt the loss very heavily. Just like they had gathered to watch the royal wedding between Prince Charles of England and a common girl, they were once again glued to their televisions, only this time to witness the official ending of a real life fairy tale.

What was it that caused such a deep sense of loss? Princess Diana had truly represented the advancement and evolution of archetypes that are inherently deep within our psyches and have been played out between the Male and Female since the dawn of time. These archetypes are common and are applied without much thought, filling societal expectations and traditional roles.

The death of Princess Diana was the beginning of the end of these roles. Diana had been a shy kindergarten teacher when she was noticed by her Prince Charming. He swept her off her feet and into a fairy tale marriage, making her a princess, with the promise of delivering romance, treasure, and some day lifting her up to become Queen. Girls, women, and fathers of daughters all watched with bated breath. It could have been one of us!

In a fairytale, all we are told is that they lived happily ever after. In real life, Diana had failed to recognize that this promise would come with a price. She was now at his beck and call and was to remain beautiful and young. No one had told her that she would have to fit the expectations and rules of the existing Queen, who was cold and calculating, profit-oriented, and driven by power. The beautiful flower was squashed and disheartened. The Prince found refuge in his long-time forbidden love to a married woman, and Diana did her best to keep face.

To distract and soothe her Self, she found romance on her own, and eventually left the kingdom and her marriage to the future King of England. Diana was well loved by the people, and through her example of taking care of her Self, being in service for charity, and using her kindness for the welfare of the commoner, she quietly became the Queen of Hearts for all of England. All on her own! A true Queen of her own making and selected by the people.

This emerged very clearly the day she became the Victim of sensationalism, and is what sent the Royal family into a frantic tailspin of ignorance and denial.

The Queen of England refused to acknowledge her ties to Diana, and no flags were raised on Buckingham Palace. No official funeral was planned until the Queen was forced to face the sea of flowers outside the palace and hear the people's angry demands for a proper treatment of their Queen of Hearts.

No one had ever reached this kind of status without going through the proper channels. Princess Diana's legacy to us is to end giving our power away to someone else. We no longer have to wait for our Prince to ride in on a horse to lift us up, only to end up at his mercy. The Prince can now truly choose his mate for love, and does not have to settle for an acceptable substitute to suit society's demands.

The grief experienced by the people that mourned the loss of Princess Diana was about the end of an era where, even though women were powerless, they could count on being taken care of. A new way of taking personal responsibility, where one stands in their own power despite the fear of judgment and possible consequential abandonment, was born. She was a pioneer, and the outcome of her courage to defy tradition should not stop anyone from following in her footsteps.

Today, all eyes are on Kate Middleton and Prince William. Would she have been better off to run instead of following in Diana's steps? Will we watch these two new humans illuminate and transform the world and show us what an equal energy relationship looks like?

They, as much as the rest of us, are invited to become balanced Kings and Queens of our own making, confident in our talents, abilities, strengths, and gifts. We can now freely share our qualities by expressing our true desires, and achieve the ultimate union as whole Beings desiring to be together and live happily ever after.

~

Some traditions hold true. "Ladies first" is more than just good etiquette. When you listen to your inner Female's voice first, you will make decisions that are based on trust and choices that feel exciting and evoke enthusiasm and joy.

Once a decision feels great, bring in your inner Male. If the two have not yet met, introduce them, and then ask him to come up with a logical, reasonable plan that makes sense. Allow the inner Female to sit with him and ask him to slow down and check to see if the plan he is creating is the easiest and most graceful way to create the best possible outcome with the least effort.

When all is considered, the inner Male can then execute the plan by taking the smoothest action to manifest the best possible outcome with guaranteed flow. As soon as you start to force or push, to get to where you would like to be, ask your Self to stop. Let your heart, your inner Female, your intuition and your inner knowing, guide you, and your inner Male will thank you for making life a more pleasant, rewarding, and relaxed affair.

Opus Lux Action Tip

Check to see if you are immersed in the archetype of a Damsel in Distress, Knight, Prince, or Princess, and upgrade your inner Male and your inner Female to rule over your kingdom in unity, as balanced King and Queen.

~Basic Needs~

"We can feel instantly peaceful within the moment, if we choose not to feel compelled to prove ourselves to others."
~Anon~

We live in a society that has taught us to depend on others to fulfill even our most basic needs. When you are in a relationship, you are asked to give what you have to fill the other person's needs, and they, in return, give you what they have to fill what you need. Neither one has exactly what the other requires, and pretty soon both are starving and deprived, blaming the other person for the lack and deprivation experienced.

If everyone filled their own needs and depended on themselves, there wouldn't be a necessity for rescuers and heroes anymore. With all needs filled, your innate cup would be full and overflowing. What overflows from you is what you give away. If everyone did this, we would live in a world of glorious abundance.

The end of the Industrial Age arrived some years ago and we are no longer just thinking about putting food on our table, a roof over our head and shoes on our children's feet. With the arrival of the Information Age, we created greater results with less effort, but failed to step out of survival mode and enjoy the extra time, money, and freedom at hand. Instead we opted to build bigger houses, buy faster cars, and push ourselves even harder than ever before to keep up with it all.

There are those whose sole purpose appears to be to provide. They are celebrated for being Selfless. With all their energy being pumped into providing, they soon become depleted and starved. Then there are those whose sole purpose appears to be to depend on those who provide. They are seen as powerless and deemed Selfish. Using all their energy to extract sustenance from others, they soon become depleted and starved. It doesn't really matter which role you pick, both being Selfless and being Selfish create lack.

~

For many years, citizens of so-called civilized nations proudly distributed bags of rice to impoverished nations like Africa. Each month the hungry recipients, now dependent on these deliveries, wondered if the helicopter would come back again and if they would have food for the next month or if they would starve.

A big shift is now taking place. You will see what true empowerment can do to a developing country filled with eager women who are utilizing the twenty or fifty dollars supplied by microloans to bead, stitch, sew and weave their way out of starvation and into a Self-reliant sustainable future.

And because they have to pay off the borrowed money - which 95% of them do - the money is invested wisely and handled with respect. In place of supplying rice, more and more rescue organizations are handing out fishing nets or simple farming tools, creating true empowerment instead of dependency.

The four basic needs are food, shelter, clothing and love.

Food:

Filling the basic need of food does not just depend on your ability to put food on your plate. How are you nurturing your Self? Do you fill your physical temple with foods that have been raised with love, natural remedies, pure water, exercise, fresh air, and a daily dose of sunshine?

Are you giving your body enough rest and consideration, or are you pushing it way beyond its natural limits, exploiting, depleting, and undermining its true potential and ability to be perfectly healthy? Are you letting the media or society fill your mind with negativity, or do you slow down long enough to discern what feeds your Soul? Nurture your Self in every conceivable way!

Shelter:

Shelter is not just about having a roof over your head. Feeling sheltered also means to feel protected, secure, and safe. Being protected is not guaranteed by having five locks on your door, iron bars on your windows, or having a million dollars in your bank account. Having a solid financial plan is very important, and having money saved for an unexpected dry spell, or building passive income to create financial freedom, can give you a sense of security. Yet, more than anything, your true protection is found in listening to your Heart voice.

It will ring an alarm, raise the proverbial red flags, and if you follow its promptings, you are safe and warned of any dangers. When you believe in your Self, cheer your Self on, and are your authentic Self, you are protected, safe, and exude Self-worth and confidence.

Clothing:

Having the ability to keep your Self protected from a sometimes harsh environment, or to be stylish and show your own personality by the design of your clothes, is only the first aspect of this basic need. Another just as important component has to do with how much you care about what others think or say.

The glory of showing your true Being and living your life in its most authentic form requires that you not break under the weight of judgment and stay true to your Self despite what others might think or say. Simply decide to be seen as who you truly are. Do what works for you, because just like Dr. Seuss said, "Be who you are and say what you feel, because those who mind don't matter and those who matter don't mind." Don't you admire the Eccentric who lives life fully by allowing himself to be interestingly different instead of being boring and dull, and, above all, doesn't care what anyone thinks or says?

Love:

Most of us have learned from example that it is wrong to love ourselves. That the sheer act of being true to our Self, is forbidden and could be interpreted as being Selfish. In our collective consciousness, being Selfless is a much more valued quality, and is enforced with diligence and false promises. Weren't we continually assured, that being humble enough to make the Self secondary, is supposed to be a sure-fire ticket to being admitted through the gates of heaven?

If you loved your Self at least as much as you loved others, you would not need anyone else's love or be dependent upon the mercy of others. You wouldn't have to work so hard to be loved. And the love, as your cup slowly fills and eventually overflows could be bestowed upon others without sacrifice or suffering.

After all, Jesus didn't teach to love your neighbor more than your Self. Buddha led his followers to find a middle path between the two extremes of Self-indulgence and Self-mortification, and what arises is a whole person who loves Self as much as others because he is aware of the oneness of all that is.

Above all, fill your own needs first!

Fulfill your own needs first. Then fulfill the needs of those for whom you are responsible. Discern between a need and a desire. Once your needs and the needs of those you are responsible for are filled, fill some of your own desires. Then fulfill some of the desires of those for whom you are responsible. Disappointment is a direct effect of an unrealistic expectation. You may not always receive your highest aspiration, but will always have what you need. What you perceive you need could vastly differ from what your Soul needs in order to grow and expand.

When you declare that you are ready for a full, happy, abundant life, you could be forced to change old behaviors, like giving too much, trusting others more than Self, or being a people pleaser, since these actions do not create the above desired result.

Was there a time in your life when you didn't have enough money to pay your rent or buy essentials? It may have been hard to ask for help, find a solution, or learn that it's okay to show your vulnerability to the world. Through these experiences you had the opportunity to become more graceful in receiving help, to admit that you might need to follow a budget, or to make changes in your career.

Opus Lux Action Tip

Always remember that if everyone filled their own needs first, we would all be full. Be the best possible example to all whose lives you touch, and then enjoy the incredible feeling of being able to give to others when your own cup starts to overflow.

~ Responsibility ~

"They were looking for an altitude-tested, deep sea-experienced, egg-laying, whole milk pig."
~Swiss saying ~

Being responsible means that you have taken full authority over your life, are accountable for what you've agreed on and have the required maturity to foresee the consequences of your actions. You are willing to not just take praise, but also the blame, should the ensuing results require it. You are in charge of what you have taken on, display follow-through, be dependable, and need to be aware that you are liable for what your choices caused.

With so much at stake, it's understandable that responsibility is not always embraced with the enthusiasm that's needed, and the burden of it can come to feel like the proverbial albatross around the neck. It is so much easier to let someone else take on the burden, as well as the glory, of responsibility. It seems that the more responsibility someone is able to hold, the more powerful they become. Those who hold it call the shots, and those who have given it away become more and more dependent on those who hold said responsibility for them.

Holding responsibility for others that can't do for themselves feels great at first. To be strong enough to carry more than your own load may make you feel superior and give you a temporary energy boost. You may have offered your help in hopes that the other person can rest and regain their own strength while you carry their backpack for a period of time. Yet you may be surprised that even if they do recover, they will usually not ask for you to return the burden to them. You are doing such a great job, and they can use their new-found energy to play, have fun, or do something else!

By taking on others' responsibilities you are also taking their power. Give them back their power!

Imagine that each baby comes with a bag of feathers. Each feather represents a responsibility. As they grow up, every time you hand them a responsibility, they are putting a new feather in their wings. First you teach them how to eat, walk, and talk. Then they learn to function in the community, dress themselves, do their own homework, clean up after themselves, make their own sandwich. Then you teach them how to scrub the toilet and the kitchen floor, run the lawnmower, cook a meal for the whole family, drive a car, get an after-school job, balance a bank account, pay for their own gas and car insurance, pay their own parking tickets, and allow them to take on more and more adult responsibilities as they mature. By the time they are grown, they are supposed to be fully feathered.

As parents, we are responsible to support, nurture, and protect our children. We carry their responsibilities until they are strong enough to carry their own, and get excited every time they accept one more feather, even if that implies that some day they will no longer need us. It is our job to make them fit for life, equip them to be functional members of our community, and then cheer them on and tell them that we believe in them. The greatest moment arrives when they spread their wings and take off in full flight.

Many parents are afraid that their youngster might crash and burn or be overburdened by being given responsibility. Some keep a handful of feathers hidden away to ensure dependency and to remain in control. Give them their feathers and watch them fly beyond your own backyard, out into the adventure of a full life!

~

We can always learn from animals. When eagles build their nests, they use their underbelly plumage to create a comfortable, soft pillow, over the structure of branches and twigs, in which to lay their eggs. Folklore has it that each time Mama Bird or Papa Bird fly off to get more food for the babies, they take one of those soft feathers with them, making the nest increasingly more uncomfortable as they grow.

By the time the eaglets are ready to fly, Mama Bird stretches out one of her wings, and the youngsters hop on it and use it as a runway to take flight for the first time. There is always a chance that one of the little birds decides that it is not quite ready to spread its tiny wings, and hunkers down in the by now incommodious nest.

If you thought the eagle parents would push their hesitant offspring out of the familiar nest, guess again. They simply feed it less and less, and eventually stop, inspiring the craven to gather its courage and seek what it needs outside of home and take its only chance to live up to its awesome potential.

Translated to human reality, this example could help stop you in your tracks and highlight the insight that sometimes less is more. Your children will not usually leave the nest until they can afford to live at least the same, if not better, lifestyle that they get to enjoy while living with you.

~

Meet Jonathan. His parents were at the end of their rope, didn't know how to get off the roller coaster ride they had been on for the past five years, and were desperate for help. Their son was afflicted with a heroin addiction, and they were afraid that he would die if they stopped catching him now.

It had started with shoplifting when Jon was thirteen. His parents paid the fine, and his mom later said that he was too young to get a job to pay them back. It had never occurred to her to ask him to mow the lawn, wash their cars, or empty the dishwasher to earn back the money his family had spent to pay for his mistake.

Next came a series of misdemeanors, minor felonies, and an unauthorized entry into a vacant property. His parents bailed him out and paid for the legal expenses. Soon it became obvious that their son was using drugs, stole money from his parents' home, and even hawked their TV to pay for it. They paid for rehab. His dad took three months off work to live with his son in a cabin in the woods to help him with the withdrawal symptoms, fight the cravings, and learn how to deal with stressful situations. The family had to put a second mortgage on the house, and eventually lost their home. Helplessness and depression settled like a shadow over their former lives. Jonathan could not withstand the vicious cycle, and gave in to the impulses the drugs had caused in his brain.

Every time his parents caught him, Jon had to fall a little further down the next time. By catching him again and again, the consequence of not letting him take responsibility for his actions increased and grew larger. In the end, the reality that Jon might die, should they decide to let him fall now, was not unfounded. Could the downfall of this family have been prevented? And if yes, then how?

Simply by giving their child the opportunity to take responsibility for the consequences of his actions from the very start would have made him aware that he is accountable and that his parents are not here to pick up his slack and give up their own lives in order to save his. Jonathan may still have a chance, but it depends entirely on the willingness of his parents to start doing less and less for him, and eventually to completely back off.

~

Ask your Self who and what you are truly responsible for. After contemplation, you may find that you are not really responsible for anyone but your Self, your growing children, plus any pets and plants that require your care.

What about your elder parent or disabled kin? Can you share the added responsibility with other family members, give the loved one in need the care they deserve, and still take care of your own responsibilities? What about your spouse? You may be legally responsible for debt incurred, and morally responsible for fair compensation if they work at home raising the children and keeping the house, but you are not responsible for his or her happiness or personal decisions and choices reached outside of mutual agreement.

Remember that taking on anyone else's burdens gives you a sense of power. You feel stronger than they, and this makes you feel needed and powerful. Realize that it is you who sucks the power right out of them when you hear your Self complain about how weak they are.

Trust that no one has ever picked more than they are capable of handling, and that everything on their plate is there to help them grow, expand, and become more of who they already are. Allow others to do all they can do for themselves, and when they ask for help, teach them what you know. Once you give back to others what truly belongs to them, you have more energy to deal with your own opportunities and challenges, and finally have enough energy to be creative and to fulfill your own life's purpose.

~

It has become a trend that whoever is willing to take on the most responsibility at work will be the one who is advanced in position, receives a higher income or more perks, and is least likely to be fired. Living in this highly competitive environment has taken its toll. A single worker is now doing a job that used to take three or four people to do. Extra shifts are added, extra responsibilities are taken on, and there is more stress, more pressure, and ever higher expectations, all in the name of greater productivity, and for the same low pay.

The readiness to be everything to everyone is sad evidence of a society that has lost direction. People sell out by doing whatever is asked, giving up free time, and agreeing to a lesser salary if only they get to keep their jobs. More people end up having high blood pressure, heart attacks, and other symptoms of the loss of joy, all because they don't have the courage to risk losing their jobs.

Those who have been laid off, fired, or are making less money due to the struggling economy, are forced to let go of some of the responsibilities they had previously taken on when money was flowing more freely. They are devastated when they realize that they can no longer afford to be responsible for the house that is much bigger than they really need, their daughter's car payment, or even drive their own car because it consumes too much gas.

Single mothers finally muster up the courage to go after the deadbeat dads of their children. Many start their own businesses, doing what they are really meant to do, sharing their true talents and turning their passions into lucrative businesses. This allows them to be their own bosses, be responsible for themselves, nurture their children, and do what they came here to do.

~

Allow others to be responsible for what they cause. Inform and educate them, show them how to fish instead of fishing for them, and by all means live by example. You cannot possibly be responsible for preventing your grown loved-one's acquisition of, say, type 2 diabetes, since they are the ones who eat too many sweets, indulge in carbohydrate-rich foods, barely get any exercise, and refuse to find out the metaphysical cause of why they do that.

It is their choices and decisions that have caused it. And you may tell them to stop complaining and do something to change it. However, bear in mind that humans are here on the plane of duality to experience cause and effect, and rarely change by being told what to do.

~

What would happen if you only helped when asked, if you only gave away what you have extra, and if you learned to ask for help for your Self when you needed it?

Opus Lux Action Tip

Make a list of all that you are responsible for. Give up all that you feel obligated to do, return what is not yours to its rightful owner, eliminate what requires too much of your energy, and be accountable for all you are genuinely responsible for.

~ Nurturing ~

"In making others happy, you will be happy too,
for the happiness you give away returns to shine on you."
~Helen Steiner Rice~

With few exceptions, all of us were born with a full cup. Having a full cup means to be filled to the brim with energy to live life fully. Each day some of that energy is used, and each day life has the potential to add energy to your cup. As you engage in activities or find your Self in situations that drain you, you lose energy from your cup, while experiences that fulfill you literally add to it.

Our culture has praised those who are Selflessly holding their cup in outstretched arms and are giving freely to those who appear to have less. The motto of giving until there is nothing left, "Here, have some of mine. You look like you have even less than I do," keeps many of us drawing from our cup until it is empty. But that's not where we stop. A truly good Samaritan will drill holes in the bottom of the cup to get into the reserves and excavate the mine until the last ounce of energy is dug up and distributed.

Those deemed Selfish are so afraid of losing energy from their cup that they hold it so close to themselves, that life cannot possibly add all it has to offer. They shelter and protect the little they have with the fierceness akin to a lioness protecting her cubs. Since they have so little, whatever they can spare from their sparse belongings feels like a lot more to them than what a Selfless person perceives as plenty.

To balance each other, it is not uncommon for givers to attract takers. And if they continue their behavior, both will eventually feel wronged, used, and taken advantage of. The giver feels like they are filling a bottomless pit from which nothing ever returns, and the taker feels overwhelmed with what he perceives as constant unreasonable demands that he can never fill, a sense of being at the mercy and beck and call of the one who has offered to help fill his barren cup. All that is left are two starving beings devoid of happiness and fulfillment.

Is the quotation by Helen Steiner Rice you find at the top of this chapter particularly deceiving, even though it sounds like a very lovely idea? Is it really true that all you have to do is "make others happy" and it will return to you?

Due to the attachment of expectation, the notion of giving to others to get something in return has created more disappointment and disillusionment than any other false belief in our collective consciousness and has caused more harm than all other lies combined!

Digging into and depleting your reserves is comparable to taking a saw to a full-grown majestic tree. Have you watched loggers sawing through the thick trunk of a tree and nervously wondered just how much further they have to cut in order for the tree to fall? And were you surprised that it didn't fall until the saw had cut through to almost the very end. And that once it falls down, you can't glue it back on, and you have to literally grow a new tree?

Regrowing your tree requires patience, nurturing, and knowhow. The old paradigm to "push way beyond your limit" is exposed as an invalid key. All pushing hard did was to burn all the energy in your cup. And then, if this was not enough, you used up all of your reserves! It's a lot like thinking that if you push hard enough, your car will go another 20 miles on an empty tank.

Unfortunately, we can't just stop by the gas station to fill up the energy we need to function properly.

Imagine that life adds a little energy to your cup each day, say 10% of the full capacity possible. To gain strength, you must use less than what you have. If your tank is empty, or less than overflowing, stop when you've used 5%, or half of what is in your cup right now, and long before you are tired. The next day life will have added a little more. If you were empty to start out with, you are now at 15%. Again use only half of the energy you have. Keep going, using only half of what is in your tank, until your cup is full and overflowing. And then, only give away what overflows from your full cup. This strategy may take a lot of willpower and could be utterly frustrating for those who have a lot of drive. Be tough with your spending habits!

It's tempting to fall into old habits, especially when you feel your energy return. This remedy is guaranteed to fill your tank with new gained energy.

You will have to choose activities, behaviors and beliefs that fill you and give up those that drain you. Look at your cup every so often, and even in high-energy times, check in to make sure you only give away what truly overflows from you. This recipe works for all empty tanks, including your financial tank.

You are filled by being who you are, doing what you love. You will learn to nurture your Self, give back responsibility to where it belongs, and stop giving more than you have. You will learn to say no when you feel too much pressure or when something feels like an obligation.

Your inner Male will fall in love with your inner Female as you introduce the two and allow them to connect and create in synergy to produce greater results with less effort. You will learn to rely on your Self to fill your own needs first and hold your cup in front of you far enough away to make sure you are not using more than you have, yet not so close as to prevent life from adding to it freely. Your cup will fill up to its full capacity and start to overflow. What overflows is what you give away, and there will be plenty to give.

~

It is often our inner Child that either misses the mother-love it experienced or is seeking the mother-love it never had from those who are now around him. Parents who have overprotected or overindulged their increasingly-weaker-growing descendants have lead their by now immobilized children into lives of dependency. Most of our parents didn't receive the nurturing they needed from their parents and either didn't realize what was missing or have overcompensated for what they didn't have when raising you. If they, themselves, were starved of nurturing, how were they supposed to know how to nurture themselves, or let alone, teach their children what it means to nurture one's Self?

What constitutes nurturing of Self, and why is it so important?

When we nurture ourselves, we fill the Self with exactly what it needs to feel whole, cared for, and loved. Once we overflow, we can pour the extra onto those who are in our care. If those in our care learn to nurture themselves, they learn to depend on themselves, are full, and can shower their loved ones with what overflows from them.

No one is starving, and what is shared is extra. Like the cherry on top or the whip cream on the already decadent cake. Once you learn to nurture your Self, you will project "I enjoy being nurtured," and before you know it, those around you will be eager to nurture you.

Nurturing Self starts with tuning in to your personal needs and desires.

If you think that all you need to nurture your Self is to take a bath once in a while, read on.

Nurturing your physical body:

Your physical body is the vehicle of your Soul. Treat it with utmost respect and care. Feed it with high-vibrational foods and pure water, let it breathe fresh air, put your bare feet in the sand, swim in the ocean, soak up some sunshine, and go for a walk in a glistening snow-covered forest. Dance, bike, climb a mountain, and strengthen your muscles, all in moderation and with the intention of connecting with the nurturing power of Mother Earth.

Pay attention to your body. It will tell you when it's tired, how much sleep it needs, and when it has sat in front of an electronic gadget or in a car for long enough.

Nurturing your mental body:

Does your inner Slave Master panic when you simply think of taking some time for your Self? Is your mental body constantly piping up with all the reasons why there is a need for more work to be done, and argues that you simply haven't given enough of your Self to those around you? Remember that you are listening to your hard-working inner Male. Slow down and remind him that you will manifest greater results with less effort if your mind is allowed to experience different impressions and benefits from a rewarding mini vacation a couple of times a day.

Replace your negative thoughts with positive affirmations whenever you become aware that you are on your Slave Driver's leash.

Nurturing your emotional body:

When you are in touch with your feelings, you are in tune with your Heart voice. The choices that best serve and please you are reflected by the degree of enthusiasm, joy, and excitement that you experience when faced with having to make a decision. Your feelings and emotions are your most accurate guide, and you can trust your Self to know exactly what feels good and what does not.

Paying attention to how you feel is a form of nurturing Self. Your choices must include considering, respecting, and honoring your Self. How often do you say, "I don't know," "I don't care," or "Whatever you choose," when you could easily consider your options and say, "I would prefer this," "This approach would serve me better," or "Let's negotiate a win-win situation"?

Nurturing your spiritual body:

Your Soul is pure love. It will rebel when faced with neglect or deprivation, and will let you know loud and clear what it needs. Feeding your Soul is easier than you think. All it desires is that you love your Self, follow your bliss, and find the gift in each situation.

Your Soul knows that you are a Light-Being having a physical experience. It knows everything that has ever been, is, and will be, and what your particular life's mission is. It will nudge, prod, and guide you. If you ignore the Soul and starve its urge to live life fully, your emotional, mental, and physical bodies will deteriorate, and your life in general will reflect the limitations and confinement caused by this blatant disregard.

~

So, draw a bath, light some candles, sip a tall glass of freshly pressed juice, relax into the soapy bubbles, and let your imagination roam freely to determine what truly feeds your Soul. Be kind to your Self, praise your Self, give your Self the same leeway you allow your best friend. You may be surprised to realize that others are watching you with a suspicion that eventually turns into hidden admiration, and they might, after some contemplation, follow your example.

Nurturing your Self first does not signify that you will now stop nurturing others. It simply demonstrates that you are responsible for your own well-being, that you consider, respect, and honor your own needs and desires, and, in return, will project, "I enjoy being nurtured."

Example: A personal account of the tragic death of Shaddai.

My first contact with Shaddai was over the phone, and even though I had never met her in person, I felt very close to her, almost as if I had known her all my life. Shaddai told me that she had been diagnosed with breast cancer, had undergone a battery of surgeries, chemotherapy, and followed her treatment plan faithfully. When doctors told her that they had done everything they could, she started to look for answers outside of traditional medicine.

I explained to her that the general metaphysical cause for breast cancer is an unconscious, deep Self-resentment over excessive giving and nurturing of others, not getting enough in return, and never having anything left for Self. What Shaddai needed to change to heal her by now considered "terminal" stage IV breast cancer was to nurture her Self with the same consideration and care she had for others, and to only give away what overflowed from her.

Those, certainly, were foreign words and concepts to her. She had grown up on a farm, was expected to lend a helping hand, and be there for her younger siblings. As the oldest daughter, she had learned that in order to be acknowledged and to receive approval, she had to relinquish her personal power, curb her individuality, and stifle her emotional needs. Her family needed and depended on her, which became her modus operandi in all of her relationships, and was how she came to give away more than she really had.

In order to save her dignity, Shaddai chose not to ask for what she desired. When she dared to express her own viewpoints or opinions, she was quickly put in her place and shut down. Being a "busy-bee" reaped most of the acknowledgment and the recognition she so craved, and this pattern led to her life-long commitment to be of service to all who touched her life. She was shocked by the idea of allowing her Self to live life with ease and grace. In our initial phone sessions, she had a really hard time wrapping her mind around the concept of giving to her Self what she desired, pouring love upon her Self, and, especially, encouraging others to fill their own needs.

Exploring her own individuality led to a quest to discover what she personally loved. "How will I dress, wear my hair, decorate my space, eat, exercise? What hobbies will I explore, which books will I read, what types of movies will I watch, if I chose what truly resonates with me and reflects who I truly am? What will I choose in order for the outer picture to truly match my inner landscape?" Those were hard questions for her to answer, and still, her will to live was greater than her fear of change. Shaddai did her best to find the answers, follow through with living them, and loved how the results made her feel.

Her greatest challenge to give up doing for others what they could do for themselves was presented by her son. No matter what she did to help him, his problems kept getting bigger and bigger. Drugs, alcohol, and loss of employment were destroying the life of her much loved charge. She struggled with the concept of tough love towards him. Shaddai did everything in her power to rescue him. She was secretly embarrassed by how he chose to live. Her labor of love did nothing but deplete her, and a feeling of having failed him started to bloom inside her aching heart.

As hard as it was for her, she gave her son back his power. She handed him back responsibility and focused on pouring love upon her Self, to be the best example she could possibly be for him. She learned to do less for others and more for her Self. Shaddai became a master of standing in her own power, nurtured her Self by making choices and decisions that pleased and served her, and learned to express her viewpoints and opinions. She made new friends and found support in different and interesting places.

Within a few short months, her blood readings and the regular tests related to the treatment of breast cancer got better and better. Her energy increased. She felt the changes she had made take effect, and her physical body started to heal. The doctor, who she described as frugal with his time and somewhat curt in manner, sat her down for an unexpected chat. He asked her what she was doing different, since he had never seen anyone recover from death's doorstep the way she had. He showed genuine interest, was open to her complementary treatments, and encouraged her to continue to apply what was working so well.

Looking at Shaddai from an energetic viewpoint, I could no longer detect cancer in her physical body. She was still weak and had a ways to go before I would consider her completely healed. Right around that time, her parents were talking about selling their farm. Plans were hatched, and they decided to move to a bigger house where Shaddai, her husband, and her parents could all live together. It felt like a big test.

Would she be able to transform her old patterns when exposed to a situation that would be very tempting and put her at risk of falling back into her destructive behaviors? She felt it was a great opportunity for her to apply her new-found knowledge, learn how to nurture her Self while nurturing others, and express her viewpoints and opinions as an adult with her elderly parents.

Her siblings and other relatives were afraid that she would be overwhelmed and do too much for her parents if they all lived together while she was still in recovery, and did their best to talk her out of it. Shaddai could not be deterred, and they found the perfect house in record time. Our phone sessions at that time were focused on tempering how much she does for others, as well as to strengthen her ability to only choose what resonates with her, even if this upsets others.

Not long after moving to the new house, her doctor strongly recommended one last round of chemotherapy as an "insurance" to make sure that all of the cancer cells were destroyed. Shaddai called me to ask what I thought about this. I told her that she had the answer in her own heart. She alone knows best what feels true to her. She said she felt that she didn't need it, but was probably going to go through with it, since her family felt that she should do what the doctor thought was best for her. I could feel that she was teetering back and forth. The burning question was: Be true to my Self, or quench the lingering fear of those who love me?

Shaddai chose to follow the fear voice. The chemotherapy completely dissolved her liver, her abdomen started to fill with water, and three weeks later she was dead. Her death certificate stated that she had died due to complications with breast cancer. I was devastated and angry. Her family, her loved ones, all her friends, the people she had touched, and all those who would never get a chance to know her, had lost an amazingly beautiful person who had filled their lives with love, kindness, dedication and wisdom.

When I was contemplating whose story I should tell for this particular chapter of this book, Shaddai made it very clear that this was her opportunity to make a difference in peoples lives. Even though she had left her physical form and could only be heard or seen by those who have a heightened extrasensory perception, her message needed to be heard. When she was still in physical form, she had given me two Angel-speak readings, a specialty she developed by connecting to the realm of angels and tuning in to the messages they had for those who needed them. I still have those beautiful reminders of Shaddai's talents and gifts, and was not surprised to be contacted by her now.

As you may have guessed, Shaddai is not the name her proud parents gave her when she was born into the world of duality. To protect her family's privacy, she told me she would like me to use her angelic name for the story, and that I would find it on the Internet. I briefly meditated, and Archangel Metatron came into view. I looked up Archangel Metatron online and found that the name Shaddai is numerically equivalent to

Metatron. The root of the word Shaddai means victorious and assertive. The Hebrew word for "breast" is shad. She who provides all our needs, just as mother's milk provides every need of a newborn!

Wow. Nothing could have described her more accurately. Archangel Metatron is known to help us find the measure for all we do. It is thought that Metatron stopped Abraham from sacrificing his son, Isaac, to God. It becomes very clear that Shaddai was here on Earth to know the difference and contrast of when enough is enough. The true measure of all the good she did and the love she gave.

Had she been more assertive, she would have been victorious. And in the most amazing way, she is. She has completed her purpose. Shaddai has become a messenger, creating a bridge between the Divine and humankind. She reminds us that each of us innately knows when we have done enough, and that we need to love and nurture ourselves as much as we do others.

~

If you feel deprived, limited by what life has to offer, and rely on others for your happiness, you will find relief as soon as you make peace with what you have right now. Count your blessings, take note of all you already have, and express gratitude for all the good in your life.

Your Soul is begging you to stop your struggle, discontinue acting like you are not good enough, thinking that there is never enough of anything, and failing to appreciate what you already have. Give up comparing your Self to others and embrace your perceived shortcomings. Take care of your old tattered car and remember all the times it transported you exactly where you needed to go. If you don't have one, be grateful that you have a bike or that you can take a bus. Spruce up your worn clothes with a few colorful accessories. Prepare your simple food offerings with love. Stop complaining, and announce that you are perfectly content with what you have.

What you resist will persist.
The fears, obstacles and challenges you embrace will disappear.

You cannot move forward until you are completely content with where you are now. Show gratitude towards all that comes your way. Express gratitude to those who give freely of what overflows from them. Always choose the best of what is offered, and offer to others what overflows from you. Fill your reserve tank and then your own cup, and remember that when it feels like you have nothing to give to your Self or others, you always have gratitude, a smile, or a kind word to share. In the following chapters, you will further discover where you lose energy, carry unnecessary baggage, and how to fill your empty spaces and various love tanks.

To nurture your Self requires that you consider, respect, and honor your Self in equal proportion to what you give to others. Encourage your Self and those in your care to nurture body, mind, and Soul. If everyone nurtured themselves, we would all be cared for, happy, content, and could freely share what will so abundantly overflow from us.

Opus Lux Action Tip

In a meditative state, visualize giving your inner Child everything she never had growing up. Throw her the birthday party she really deserved. Dress her in a beautiful outfit, put a crown on her head, hand her a magic wand. Shower her with presents, delicious foods, play games, cuddle, and horse around with her before you give her a bath. Tell her a good-night story, rock her to sleep, and sit by her bed all night to guard and protect her. Tell her that she can ask for anything she desires, and that you will always be there for her. You will be amazed at her transformation and happy to see the glowing, contented smile on her face.

~ Acceptance ~

"Be who you are and say what you feel,
because those who mind don't matter
and those who matter don't mind."
~Dr. Seuss~

The difference between tolerance and acceptance is profound. When we tolerate something, we are far from being at peace, and we experience an emotional charge which incidentally proceeds to eat at our very substance and just so happens to feed our metaphorical "black dog."

Judgment:

When judgment is involved, we see that others are different, feel that they are bad or wrong, and have a great need that they change. Often we invest a good amount of energy into focusing on what we think others need to change; battling, fighting, arguing, and challenging them so they will come to their senses and see our point.

This kind of attitude then turns into an approach that leaves room only for "It's my way or the highway" and is caused by thinking that we have found the key to the one and only truth. We have fallen into the trap of the belief that there is only one right way and one absolute truth, and that everyone who does not see it this way is wrong, bad or ignorant.

Discernment:

Discernment, on the other hand, is to see that others are different and leave it at that. They are just interestingly different, and there is no urgent need for anyone to change. The difference shows us what does not work for us, and we can choose to be grateful for the opportunity to learn through observation, and come closer to knowing what actually would work for our personal needs, regardless of what others do, live by, or might model.

You can silently say, "Thank you for showing me actions that create consequences and results that would not work for me or be desirable to me." This approach will sharpen your ability to make choices and decisions that serve and please you in a short amount of time, allowing you to foresee the consequences of your actions simply by observing what others create through their actions.

Remember that each action has a consequence and a result, and that the same action will always create the same consequence and the same result.

~

If you can barely tolerate a person, group, or institution, it may be best to recognize that they are so different from you that you are on complete opposite sides. Sharing your ideas, your viewpoints, or way of life with those who are so distinctly unlike you may leave you feeling unheard, misunderstood, or even threatened. By being on the opposite side of the spectrum, they provide you the opportunity to see clearly how wonderfully perfect it is for you to be who you are, and to be comfortable with where you stand.

Without them, you may not fully understand just how much you love your own way of living life, and you could be grateful for being shown the contrast. After all, we are here on the plane of duality to experience opposites and eventually bring them into balance. Your opposition has the opportunity to become a little bit more like you, while you have the chance to become slightly more like them.

Do your best to understand why they are the way they are. If so inclined, study their background, consider everything they've experienced and what led them to the beliefs they hold. Understanding the "why" allows you to accept them unconditionally without having to agree. Hate breeds hate, so go where you are invited and stay away from where you cause too much controversy or disruption. If you feel a need to push, push gently. Share your viewpoint with those who are open to it, those who have the potential to grow from what you have to offer, and those who are lined up with your own energy.

What if it's a friend or family member that causes you to question their behavior, attitudes, or beliefs? If you feel strongly about it, go ahead and express to them what does not work for you. This gives both parties a choice and clears the air. Telling others how you feel allows them to either change or to continue what works for them, even if it doesn't work for you.

Make sure you make it about you, not them. Say, "I have a hard time being around someone that drinks alcohol, and ask you to come over to see me only when you are sober." If they decide to continue what does not work for you, you can either learn to accept them exactly the way they are, set firm boundaries or you may have to move on. This will strengthen your important relationships and clear away those that no longer matter or don't serve you anymore.

If a safe environment is guaranteed, and you experience a case of what may be unintentional child or animal abuse, ask the person causing the pain in an honest and loving way if they understand the ramifications of their conduct. When you encounter what feels like or is regarded as child or animal abuse, or you observe anyone else being violated or harmed, getting involved can be dangerous. One of the most effective choices is to call the authorities, report the incident, and let them handle the conflict.

Consider that we all have interestingly different viewpoints and opinions. A homeless person's dream may not be to have a solid roof over their head, a steady job with a retirement plan, and a Christmas bonus. They may actually love being free of the burdens that come with these kinds of responsibilities and could be completely content with being on the road. Why should they change if they are happy? Have you asked those who live and think differently if they are happy? And if they are not, what they could change? Most have the answers to that question, and all they need is someone who believes in them and cheers them on. Have you noticed that when someone tells you what to do, all it does is create resistance and antagonism?

Stop for a moment and consider what others are saying about you. Are you resisting something they say just because you don't feel like being told what to do, or do they actually have a valid point? Considering what others have to say is valuable and can lead to important and necessary changes. Make sure you only take with you what resonates and let the rest go.

~

Only by seeing both sides of the coin are we able to discern our own truth. Being immersed in duality allows us to compare, analyze, see the contrast, the differences, and make choices and decisions that work for each of us individually.

I make choices and decisions about me that serve and please me and allow others to make choices and decisions about them that serve and please them.

Example: A personal account of true acceptance.

The first friend I made when I moved to America was a woman who had the courage to pack her four young children into a tiny car with only the few belongings she was able to squeeze into the spaces between bodies and metal. She had driven far across the land to escape from religious restrictions, a husband who was abusive, and with the determination to create a better life in California.

She worked very hard for their survival, loved her adorable kids, and was there for them in every way she could be with what little she had, and still managed to have enough room in her heart to become my friend. She sacrificed so much, had the strength to educate her Self, and became a role model for many in her chosen profession. I love her to pieces and admire her greatly to this very day, more than twenty-seven years later.

The only "sore" spot in our relationship was that she is a devout Christian and desired that I take Jesus into my heart so that I will be saved. I, on the other hand, worked hard to make her see and understand that each of us, and everything around us, is divine. Not just Jesus. We really did our best to convince one another of our individual truths, and I found in me a rising ambition to not give up on her, so that one day she could see how worthy she really is.

It started to wear on our friendship, and one day we decided that we had to stop the insanity and just accept our differences. She would accept my views and support me unconditionally, while I would accept her views and support her unconditionally, without having to agree.

We are, after all, just interestingly different, and her beliefs do not take away from who I am, nor do mine take away from her. Each of us gets to live our truth in peace, and I love her even more for her willingness to embrace me even though I'm not living her truth. She is the one who has taught me the difference between tolerance and acceptance, and for that alone she will always have a special place in my heart.

This also taught me that, in order to accept, I have to understand. Looking at why someone is doing what they are doing, how they choose to live, or the beliefs they hold about themselves or their environment, has helped me to understand. Better than ever before I can now understand my mom's choices which had brought me so much pain and agony in the past. Both of her parents were cold-hearted, detached, and demanding. She grew up in the midst of World War II. She lost her husband to cancer and was saddled with poverty and physical illness.

All of a sudden I could truly understand why it was hard for my mother to nurture me, to give me affection and loving kindness, when I was growing up. She did the best she could do with what she knew and had, even though I may not have agreed with all the choices she made. I finally truly understood why she made those decisions, and simply agreed to disagree, which gave me an opportunity to make interestingly different choices and decisions for my Self, with full awareness of the contrast, and with gratitude and inner knowingness that I can apply to different actions to create a different outcome.

I do not have to agree to understand. When I understand, I can accept. And when I accept, I can love unconditionally.

It's easiest to apply this concept to people or situations which are removed from us. The closer the friendship or relationship is, the harder it is to apply. The ultimate challenge is to be understanding, accepting, and unconditionally loving towards our Selves.

If you are aggravated, disappointed, or in disagreement with someone or something, you have the opportunity to discern what does not work for you, decide what does, and put that into action. Looking at what you would like them to be, and doing exactly that for your Self, is the key. Focus back onto your Self and ask your Self if what bothers, irritates, or hurts you is something which you still do to your Self. What annoys you is possibly an attitude you, your Self, display towards others, or you may have gone too far to the opposite side and could benefit from becoming a little more like the opposition. If for example, you find it intolerable to be around an arrogant know-it-all, your Soul may crave to become just a tiny bit more like him. You could see this as an invitation to step away from the wallpaper you normally blend in with so well, and boldly announce your own viewpoint and opinion.

Does this mean you have to interact and spend a lot of time with others who are very different from you or remain in situations that show you who you are not? No. Choose to surround your Self mostly with people who are like minded and have similar goals. When challenged by family or close friends, ask them if they are willing to lay down the hatchet, forget about the differences, and celebrate what you have in common, to maintain and enjoy your bond. Stop defending your Self and become confident in just being your Self. As soon as you allow your Self to be who you are, you project "I am perfect exactly as I am" in big, bold, energetic letters, and others will treat you accordingly.

Opus Lux Action Tip

Celebrate your differences as much as what you have in common. Practice asking your Self why someone is acting the way they are so you can understand them. Once you know why, it is easy to accept them exactly the way they are and to unconditionally love them even if you disagree.

~Forgiveness~

"No snowflake in an avalanche ever feels responsible."
~Voltaire~

Forgiveness requires a release of blame. To release blame may suggest that you have to be okay with the conduct of the one who betrayed you or caused you pain. Faced with this conundrum, you might be tempted to push down your true emotions, pretend that they have disappeared, or admit that you simply cannot condone the actions of the perpetrator. You could end up holding a grudge and experiencing bitterness or resentment that results not just in a general loss of joy for life, but can literally eat up your liver, grow stones in your gallbladder, and generate heart disease.

The secret to authentic forgiveness correlates directly with the ability to find the gift in the insult or injury to your physical, mental, or emotional well-being. Finding the gift is what gives you the power to release blame and forgive those who have caused you pain.

Dedicate a space and time to meditate on the value of your experience. Visualize stepping out of your physical body, entering into the non-physical realm where you were before you incarnated into the most complex form on planet Earth, and see your Self at the long-ago gathering with all the other Souls that would enter your life for specific reasons and at specific times. With your inner vision, zero in on the scene.

You were surrounded by your guides, guards, angels, teachers, and others of the other realm to create a plan for your current life. Among other things, this plan most likely included being betrayed, cheated, judged, robbed, and lied to, so that you could experience who you are not and would find the opposite, the difference and contrast to who you truly are—an amazing Light-Being having a physical experience in the world of duality on planet Earth.

Find the diamond in the rubble.

If you could bring your Self to imagine that you may have asked to experience being wronged, you gain the power to step out of the Victim role and shift the blame away from the culprit to your Self. Now, why in the world would you have a desire to experience such pain, hurt so deeply, and, in the end, take full responsibility for what happened? Because there is a gift in it. And once you come upon the gift, it may be so grand that you discover that it was absolutely worth going through the pain to find it!

You may have asked to be betrayed so you can learn to trust your Self and follow your inner knowing at all times - even if it appears to be impractical or inconvenient to others.

You may have asked to be cheated on so you could know what it really means to respect your Self.
You may have asked to be judged so you can know what it means to be confident in your authentic Self - even if you are interestingly different than everyone else.
You may have asked to be robbed so you can learn that you are entitled to, and need to claim what is rightfully yours.
You may have asked to be lied to so that you can learn how important it is to be honest – not just with others but also with your Self.

The Villain is showing you how not to be with your Self and others.

Example: A personal account of forgiveness.

I was so excited when my best friend from the old country had finally made it to California for a visit. We had a great time, starting right where we had left off. And due to our deep friendship and love, I felt safe to embark on a business enterprise with her to export unique works of art crafted by a local artist to my native homeland.

A contract was written and signed and a plan of action discussed. We each paid half of the production and shipping costs, and I could not wait to see how quickly the pieces would find their new owners. Every time I asked my friend how the sales were going, I was told that nothing had sold yet.

After a few months, I remember having a strong feeling that I needed to do something. I thought maybe I need to call my oldest sister, ask her to pick up my half of the investment, and have her sell them in her business. But then I allowed my fear-based voice to dissuade me. This voice was telling me that should I make such a drastic move, my friend would get upset and not love me anymore. So I let it go and pretended that it was okay and told myself that some day my friend would sell the pieces and pay me my share.

Eleven years later, I was cleaning up all remaining past, unresolved business in an effort to clear my emotional blocks to prosperity. At the time, I actually really needed some money, and felt it was time to confront this particular conflict. I called my friend. We shared all kinds of developments, news and happenings in our lives, and then I took the courage to ask her about the investment I had made with her. She said that she didn't know exactly how many of the art pieces were still left, that she would check and let me know. I stated that it would be fair to get at least my investment back, and was promised to receive such within two weeks of our conversation. My friend assured me that no matter what happened now, to always remember that she loved me.

Nothing happened. When I called again, I was told that half of the pieces were left and I could pick them up at her residence, ten thousand miles from were I lived, pay a storage fee, and that she was not responsible for me. End of story.

My half had sold, was lost, or may have been given away, and I was supposed to pick up the half she had chosen to keep, all the way across the Atlantic Ocean and pay a storage fee???? My jaw dropped to the ground, my heart broke into pieces, and I felt an agonizing pain spread throughout my whole Being. I had lost what I had until then considered my very best friend! I felt betrayed, cheated, judged, robbed and lied to.

All I could hear were the following words, which she had said in our last conversation, "No matter what happens now, always remember that I love you." Apparently those who love you the most are those who are willing to hurt you the most!

I immediately started the healing process by imagining the two of us as two Soul cells, living in the non-physical realm, surrounded by love and light, expertly crafting a plan for what is now our current life experience as Light-Beings having a physical experience. No doubt, I had asked her to show me how not to be to my Self and others in all the ways described above.

Because of her I have learned how important it is to trust my Self, follow through with being true to my Self no matter what the consequences, allow my Self to have an interestingly different viewpoint or contrasting opinion, claim what is rightfully mine within a reasonable time frame, and be honest with my Self. Those are gifts so precious that they far outweigh any money I could have made, and even though it hurt at first, I had to admit that even her remark that she is not responsible for me is true in its essence.

Many times over the next two years I felt the pain rise to the surface and sting me, and every time I sat with it for a little while and reminded my Self of the gifts I'd gained. I still love my friend. She has given me so much more than I bargained for, and I am truly grateful. I was able to forgive her by stepping out of the Victim role, and was able to forgive my Self because the gifts I found have changed my life. I am no longer the same person. I feel empowered and confident.

By now the pain has given way to gratitude, and I like the idea of us sitting together, when we return to the light, slapping each other gently on the back, and congratulating each other for a job well done. I can hear us say, "We played our roles so well, we thought it was real." I am no longer a prisoner of what took place. Thank you for the gifts!

~

When you were born into physical form, you donned heavy veils, and therefore no longer remembered the reasons why you have entered into the realm of duality. At birth, you, like most other babies, still had the innate knowing of being pure and perfect. Your energy field was intact. You had confidence, felt secure, expected to be nurtured, and looked forward to this intriguing adventure into foreign lands.

Depending on your individual programming and past life experiences, you may have been shocked by the void created by the part-time absence of light in the world of duality. One moment you felt warm, nurtured and loved, and the next abandoned, unheard and deprived. Those who had given you life were now sucking it right out of you. They took away some of your joy, made you responsible for their misery, or took their frustration and anger out on you.

They needed to fill their own "holes," and, in the process, poked holes into your energy field. You had what they needed and didn't know that you had a choice as to whether to give them your confidence, your talent, your beauty, or sense of security. You were at their mercy. Just as they had been at the mercy of their parents, siblings, teachers, friends, and others in their communities who had learned to pounce on one another to get back from outside of themselves what they had lost to those around them. And those who had what you needed were going to suffer under your reign, be that your own child, your best friend, or your beloved husband.

As a child, you did not have a choice. You couldn't just say, "I'm packing my bags and I'm leaving to find me a home where I will be safe from those who rob me of my dignity, my trust in myself, and feeling acknowledged." You were stuck, at their mercy. And even if you had a nurturing home, you could not get away from the bully at school, the teacher who gave you a lower grade than you deserved, or the priest that told you that God had forgiven you for your perceived sins but you were, nevertheless, damaged goods.

Being a child often sets you up for loss. Being at someone's mercy may have left you feeling powerless and small. What a perfect set-up for knowing who you are not so that you can know who you truly are! Becoming a grown up means that you've learned to take care of all your needs, to fill your own holes from within, and regained what you've lost and given away along the way.

You now realize that you were an innocent when you first started your journey down the rabbit hole, only to find your Self in a strange wonderland that was a far cry from what you knew in your existence as a pure Being of love. As an innocent, you may have seen only the best in each person, only the good in each situation, and you may have believed that if you are a good and loving Being, that goodness will be returned, and that everyone is keeping the Highest Good of all involved in mind and heart.

How disappointing to walk innocently along the path, fall into a bear trap, and have the hyenas feast on you as they laugh at you from their high perch above. Expecting something great to happen and instead finding your Self being tricked, wronged, or betrayed erodes your innate knowing that you are a pure Being. Slowly but surely doubt seeps in. Every time you fall into another trap, your thoughts of being unworthy of anything good increase. You start thinking that there must be something wrong with you, that this would not have happened if you were special. After all, you may just be a lowly being and deserve to be punished.

It never occurs to you that you, as an innocent pure Light-Being, are experiencing these awful painful emotions and situations so that you can learn to walk safely on the plane of duality. To discern between your Ego voice and your Heart voice and truly know the difference. To lose your dignity so you can know how special you truly are. To feel insignificant and small so you can understand your true significance and importance. To protect your Self from the harm caused by the absence of light in the lower vibrational world of duality.

Only what we lose can be truly understood and appreciated once it returns. Our holes can only be filled from within, and we are here heavily veiled, under contract to play the roles of the Villain, the Rescuer, the Victim and the Saboteur, so each and every one of us can become aware of who we are and who we are not.

You will no longer take offenses personally. You will learn to protect your Self by listening to your inner alarm system and be able to recognize a perpetrator from three miles away once you step outside of the Victim role and step back into your own power. Without the absence of light, you would not know the light. And by finding the diamond in the rubble, you can truly forgive.

Forgive and never forget!

Pretending that betrayal is okay is not needed when you recognize that you were too trusting of others, and your gift is to know from deep inside of you that you can really only trust your own inner knowing. It's easier to forgive when you imagine that you asked the other person, on a Soul level, to judge you so you could know what it truly means to not just be accepting of others, but to accept your Self exactly the way you are – even if you are interestingly different from anyone else. After you let the other person off the hook, the next step is to forgive your Self for asking to be hurt.

Once you find the gift, you may love it so much that you find it possible to say that it was worth going through the pain to find it. So, forgive others and your Self, but never forget. Taking on the elephant's fabulous trait of remembering each insult, instead of ignoring the now obvious red flags and signs that lead up to the event of falling into the metaphorical bear trap, increases your understanding of duality and improves your ability to protect your Self from further damage.

Be mindful to remain open to life, and refrain from going into panic at the first sign of trouble. You now know what a "bear trap" looks like and can effortlessly avoid it. Recognizing danger erases fear, increases trust in Self, and enhances your inner knowing that your perceived mistakes have made you wiser and more of who you are. Armed with this recipe, there is no need for revenge or retribution, and you end up with an amazing gift!

~

Should you, on the other hand, find your Self as the one being accused of wrongdoing, slow down for a moment to take inventory before you start defending your Self. It is definitely more challenging to take on the role of the Villain than it is to be the Victim. The Villain has ultimately more to lose than the Victim. He is bound to be deprived of his reputation, his place in society, and quite often sacrifices his happiness.

The sufferer often feels so victimized that they seek revenge or retaliation over the grievance and are looking to instill the same harm upon the perpetrator. The Victim seldom takes responsibility for their part in the unfolding of the events, and only in rare cases does the Villain acknowledge the pain they've caused.

If you are the Villain, look at what you were seeking to gain from outside of you. Did you exploit or rob the one that has chosen to play the Victim role of their sense of security, feeling carefree, being pure, filled with joy, to fill your own empty holes? Did you notice that the feeling of finally having filled what was missing inside of you, by taking it away from someone who had what you were after, last only a short while? How quickly did your emotional body reject the infusion of positive energy stolen from someone else? Was it worth it?

It can be addictive, and the only way to heal is to become whole from within. Give your Self what others took from you. Create feeling secure from within by listening to your inner alarm system. Give back responsibility that isn't yours in order to gain a sense of being more carefree. Forgive your Self for past mistakes and start making choices that fill you with joy.

Ask the Victim for forgiveness. Acknowledge their pain, even if you see the events from a different viewpoint. The act of recognizing that they caused the pain, even if never intended or planned, is the most soothing balm on the wounds caused by the offender. Listen closely to what the Victim lost and, instead of defending your Self, apologize and say, "I am so very sorry for the feelings of grief/humiliation/abandonment, etc., I've caused you," and "Can you find it in your heart to forgive me?"

The line between Villain and Victim can be blurred. Victims become Villains and vice versa. Have you ever wondered why someone is attacking you? What did you take away from them? As a nation, what did we take away from those who now terrorize us?

If we took a good look at what led up to the wars fought in the past and present, could we possibly understand why we are so angry with one another, acknowledge the pain we've inflicted, learn from our mistakes, and communicate agreements that allow everyone involved to be understood and heard, even though we are interestingly different? We may not know the harm we've caused others until we listen with interest and an open mind. After all, there is more than one truth and more than one way to celebrate life on the planet of duality. We are supposed to be different! How boring would this place be if we all had the same experience?

~

Set personal boundaries when your inner alarm goes off and briefly slow down to recognize what exactly is about to happen. Honor the insight that it is your choice to give away your power, your joy, or your stability, and silently thank everyone involved for showing you that you can count on your Self to know what ultimately works for you. Forgive your Self and others, and erase blame, to find the disguised gift!

Opus Lux Action Tip

Free your Self from your own prison by forgiving your Self and others. This task becomes especially rewarding when you look for, and find, the gift in each experience!

~ Relationships ~

"Soul-mates are people who bring out the best in you -
they are not perfect but are always perfect for you."
~Author Unknown~

Your outer relationships are a direct reflection of your inner world. If you tend to suppress your inner Female and put a lot of emphasis on the qualities of your inner Male, don't be surprised if you find the same to be true on the outside. On the other hand, you may attract a very feminine man if you are a female who relies on her Male side a bit too strongly or a very Heart-based, intuitive partner if you mostly depend on your logic and reasoning.

Opposites attract, and if you find your Self falling in love with someone that is very different from you, know that your Soul is urging you to become a little bit more like the other person, and they have an opportunity to become more like you. Eventually those differences you thought were interesting, or, at the very least, kind of cute in the beginning start to become contentions, and over the course of time lead to a need within you that the other person change. The battle starts, the swords are raised, the rift deepens, and the ensuing war leaves all involved bloody and tired.

Once the warriors have no strength left, they need to choose if they are too beaten and must move on or if they have it in them to lick their wounds and agree to accept their opponent exactly the way they are. Your only option left is to change your Self and be surprised at how quickly your entire environment responds to your transformation.

As you get older, you may choose individuals who are more like you, who share common ground, have similar values, matching morals, can relate to your spiritual and political viewpoints, and simply complement you. In the past, you may have chosen your partners by their physical or chemical attraction, and watched as what you thought you desired turned into something that didn't work for you, showing you who you are not and how not to be in a relationship.

With each "failed" relationship, you learned more about you and what you really are looking for. If you felt ignored, in the long run you learned that, in order to get attention, you must stop ignoring your own needs and desires. All that you didn't have growing up, or lost along the way to those around you, you may have searched for in your primary or romantic relationship.

~

Thinking that the primary or romantic relationship is supposed to fill all of our love tanks is not only dangerously misleading, but downright impossible. Your love tanks are like a fuel tank in a car and need to be filled again and again. Invent more love tanks or change the content in each of them until you have your own perfect mix. You are no longer at anyone's mercy to receive the love you deserve, and it is within your own power to fill your love tanks with exactly what you need.

Here are a few general ideas on what the different love tanks represent:

Parent love tank:

Determine what you are looking for from a parent. Fill the need for parental love with a chosen substitute if you no longer have your own parents or they are physically, mentally, or emotionally unavailable.

Sibling love tank:

The rivalry may have softened and by now you have become powerful allies that share confidential information and cheer each other on. Find a substitute if you don't have a sibling that is available or interested in the kind of exchange you may seek.

Children love tank:

Many adults have a desire to take responsibility for someone that depends on their loving care or guidance and engage in carefree playfulness with the little one, who in turn provides them with a more innocent view of the sometimes harsh world we live in. If you don't have your own children, spend time with your nieces, nephews, your friends' kids, or volunteer to be part of the "Big Brother - Big Sister" program. There are so many kids of all ages who need understanding, a guiding hand and some TLC – give them the love you may never have had when you were growing up.

Friends and Associates love tank:

Networking can lead to valuable connections and support you in a multitude of circumstances.

Best friend love tank:

Benefit from having one or two very special friends who you can call in a crisis, safely share your deepest secrets with, enjoy a fulfilling reciprocal exchange of ideas, find solutions, and experience great fun with while following your passions.

Primary/Romantic love tank:

Growing up, Dad, Mom or Guardian function as our primary relationship. Choosing a romantic relationship as an adult frequently leads to looking for someone who gives us what we didn't get from our first primary relationship. Romantic relationships thrive on intimacy, love-making, enjoying each other's company,exchanging ideas, reciprocal affectionate nurturing, sharing adventures, and laughing together. These mergers ideally create synergy, a feeling of being supported, have the potential to bring children into being, and have a greater risk than any other form of relationship to be a breeding ground for expectations, disappointment, betrayal, and grief.

Animal love tank:

Each animal has at least one particular trait that people are drawn to. Dogs are loyal companions who are eager to please and have a similar therapeutic effect on their human friends as their more independent and less trainable kitty-cat counterparts. They instinctively know when you need their magical healing power, as well as how to manipulate you into scratching their bellies or taking a break to play. Determine size, specific traits, cost, and execution of care before taking on the responsibility of a Being whose welfare completely depends on you.

Intellectual love tank:

You may have special interests that can only be nurtured and fostered by someone with a high interest in what stimulates you intellectually. This love tank may require that you go outside of your main relationships and join or form a club or social organization.

Creative love tank:

Even though you might be the only one in your family or relationship who craves creative or artistic expression, make sure you cultivate this aspect with those who have similar interests. Whether you play music in a band, read your own poetry at the open mic night, build theater sets or carve sculptures doesn't matter. What mattersis that you do what fills you as an integral part of your life, no matter how much work is piling up or what others think or say.

Sports love tank:

It is highly rewarding to have a friend, or be part of a team, that matches your skill, dynamic, and strength. Spend some time being challenged, even if ever so slightly, to grow and expand your physical abilities, and then have fun teaching the kids or going at the pace of your spouse.

Spiritual love tank:

Find those who match your own spiritual or religious beliefs, share your wisdom, insights and love where you are invited and with those who make you feel at home.

Fun love tank:

Make sure you engage with those who have a sense of humor. The amount of silliness you allow into your life oftentimes directly correlates with the amount of happiness present. Moments of being carefree and playful, register high on the Richter scale and disrupts any accumulation of tension, releases built-up stress, and discharges accumulated anger.

Adventure love tank:

You can only have true adventure when you risk looking like a fool, expose your true Self, love deeply, dream big, or share your ideas with others, even if they might end up disagreeing.

Understand that if you risk nothing, you will end up with nothing. Seek the company of those who go out into the world to make a difference, create your own "bucket list," and have the courage to step outside your comfort zone and live a little.

Business love tank:

Rewarding partnerships in business rely heavily upon equal energy exchange, the amount of synergy created, shared vision, and complementary talents. Integrity and common values lay a good foundation for those who aspire to create win-win situations and cooperation. Good business partners are aware of the adverse consequences of competition, and instead look for ways to advance through cooperation, collaboration, and aiming for mutual progress.

~

Be mindful and aware of what draws you to a particular partner. Do they have something you need? Do they have more resources than you and look appealing because you could unload upon them all those heavy responsibilities that weigh you down? Are you looking for someone who will nurture you back to health after you've expended all of your own energy rescuing others? Or are you looking for the Prince promised by childhood fairy tales?

Ideally, you would learn to fill your own basic needs before even considering a committed, serious relationship. Taking full responsibility for your own life means that you've learned to make decisions that please and serve you, and you are capable of carrying the consequences of those choices with ease and grace. Your inner Male and inner Female have met and are working together beautifully -- creating the synergy that is possible when you connect Heart and Mind.

Successful relationships are based on a union between two whole Beings. Each of you can stand on your own two feet, is relying on your own talents and strengths, and accepts your Self exactly the way you are. You would not be looking for someone who will rescue you, but someone who will freely share what overflows from them. Since you already have a full cup, the extra will feel like dessert, true abundance, and, best of all, be free of charge. In return, you give what overflows from you to complement and enrich your partner's life.

The days when the Knight rescued the Damsel in Distress are over. The Prince is no longer solely responsible for delivering romance and treasure while the Princess, in return, has to remain forever young and at his beck and call. We are now asked to be Kings and Queens honoring each other's qualities and working hand-in-hand.

~

Human behavior demonstrates that we show our love in different ways. What you favor is usually closely related to what you were given as a child, or is exposed as a craving for what was lacking. Observe your loved ones to determine how they show their love. Ask what they like and tell them how you would like to be celebrated.

Being in touch with your own preference, and also considering and acting on your loved one's cherished choice, enhances mutual understanding and deepens feeling appreciated and loved.

Domestic tasks:
Cooking a special meal, surprising someone with a newly painted bathroom, a handcrafted gift, or washing their car unexpectedly, are all ways of showing love.

Gift giving:
If you spend hours finding the perfect gift for others, or have no limits on how much something costs, you may be among those who also love to receive gifts that either show how valuable you are to your admirer or how well the gift giver knows you.

Quality time:
Some much prefer spending quality time with their loved one, watching a movie or going on a hike together, and would really rather have you be with them instead of waiting alone while you are in the store looking for a gift. Shared adventures and experiences are the ultimate gift for those who thrive on connection and togetherness.

Touch:
Physical affection is mostly reserved for intimate relationships, but everyone needs loving touch. Hugs, a reassuring pat on the back, or your warm comforting hands holding those of someone lonely, sad or desperate express that you care. Pampering your loved one with nurturing touch is essential for a healthy intimate relationship, creating a deep connection between Souls, and healing emotional wounds. This form of showing love requires insight and grows more intimate the closer you become. Being respectful of different customs or the degree of desire to be touched needs to be taken into consideration. If your child is taught to be cautious with strangers,

don't ask him to submit him Self to being covered with kisses by an aunt he has never met before.

~

Have you wondered if there is only one Soul-mate for each person, and worried that you gave away your one good ticket when you split up with your first true love? Or do you have doubts that you will ever find the "one" in the midst of all of humanity if you haven't found what you are looking for yet?

In our society, marriage was invented to increase the survival of the clan and was designed to be for life – until death do you part – at a time when people only lived to be thirty to forty years old, and it was more of a necessity to get married than a choice based on mutual love.

According to the bible, when God united Adam and Eve in the Garden of Eden, he emphasized that they become one flesh and stick together. Did that really mean that once married these two should always be bound together? Or was God relating to the fact that if you separate mind and heart, look at science apart from spirituality, or disconnect one gender's qualities from the other and call it worthless, things would go bad? Was his warning saying, that separating the Male qualities from the Female qualities would be the downfall that creates imbalance, fosters and grows opposites, and if left unchecked, will undoubtedly lead to disease, miscommunication, and war?

Which is exactly what happens when logic is put above intuition or when the active principle of work and effort is worth more than the passive element of rest and rejuvenation. Is the lesson to emphasize the importance of seeing value in both sides of the coin and combine them to create synergy?

Look at any couple you know and you will see that as a whole they have the perfect amount of equal Male and Female energy. When you separate them and put one person on one side and the other on the opposite side, you will notice that if one of them has more Male energy, there is an abundance of Female energy on the other side. It's also possible that both partners have a perfectly balanced, equally developed, inner Female and inner Male. Then, as a whole, they always have equal parts of Male energy and Female energy.

If you need more Male energy, you might automatically be drawn to a partner that has a lot of Male energy, and they, in turn, could use some of the excess Female energy that overflows from you. You may now realize that you are with this person in order to become more of who they are. They, too, have an opportunity to become more like you. If one of you changes, the other one has to change, too. As you take on more Male energy, you have to give up some of your excessive Female energy. Your partner may not take on what you are giving up, and remain in the dominant Male energy. If he cannot change, and the two of you continue to stay together, the ensuing imbalance creates so much disruption that a war breaks out and disease occurs. When you no longer have a perfect balance between your Male and Female energies in your partnership, and remain in the relationship over a long period of time, one of the two Souls will usually leave by passing on.

Let's say you are hyperactive due to stress and your true nature is craving a little serenity and calmness. Will you be drawn to someone who you might call boring and too passive after you, your Self, have calmed down in their presence? You probably don't understand what attracted you like a moth to the light, and, after a while, could find it unbearable to stay with someone that you see as increasingly more dull and by now find tedious. This is when it's time to move on. Unless, of course, the calm one has picked up what you left off and integrated some of the activities you shed into his, or her, own life.

The more balanced you are, the more balanced the partner you attract.

These days, relationships come in all forms and shapes, and you are probably more realistic to promise to be with your chosen one until the relationship no longer serves either one of you, than to stay in one that kills you from the inside out.

At this point in evolution, you are more likely to see each relationship with each Soul you meet as part of your Divine plan—every single one for a specific reason and for the length of time it takes to fill a need and give you what they came to bestow upon you. There are those who are in your life to stay for a little longer so you can learn to share and grow, those who have promised to fill you with sorrow, and those who bestow incredible joy, while others hold big life-altering experiences that can take a whole life span to unfold and come to full bloom.

Opus Lux Action Tip

In the new energy, true partnerships of every kind require whole Beings who preserve their individuality even as they unite. Read "The Wedding Vows" from Conversations with God by Neale Donald Walsch for an inspiring look at a healthy commitment applicable to any partnership.

~ Swiss Cheese ~

"Through difficult experiences,
life sometimes becomes more meaningful."
~Dalai Lama, Tenzin Gyatso~

Observing the reactions of those who have just witnessed the birth of a new baby, or when they see a newborn for the first time, is tremendously rewarding. They are awestruck with the miracle of new life, dazzled by the immaculate perfection of this innocent Being, and often feel an overwhelming urge to protect, nurture and love this vulnerable little bundle of joy.

It's as if everyone is hyper-alert and aware of the ramifications of being born into the world of duality. Here Light-Beings wear heavy veils, and the absence of light creates dark and dangerous places designed to experience loss. This world is a hazardous place for such a flawless, beautiful creature!

Many parents and guardians set out to fiercely protect their charge from harm and then beat themselves up when their efforts fail while others start robbing the child's emotional body of its innocence right away. Those who are truly balanced know that it is their responsibility to keep the little one safe, yet, at the same time, allow him to fall on his nose, learn the risks of this world, and, through experiencing his own mistakes, gain the gifts of foresight and wisdom.

~

You came into this world with an intact, fully-loaded emotional body, all that you truly are in your highest form assembled like a finished picture of puzzle pieces. Each piece representing an aspect of your glory, all parts of the whole, gathered and ready to be given or taken away to find out who you are not, so that you can know when you are being all that you are and see the difference.

You are filled with Creator energy, a Light-Being having a physical experience in the world of duality where it is possible to encounter the difference and contrast to who you truly are. You are here to lose your confidence, your security, your trust, your innocence or your stability, and will gather evidence of what it feels like to lose belief in your Self, become insecure, feel betrayed, become corrupted, and know uncertainty.

Each time you lose a part of who you truly are, a hole is created in your emotional body. As you give away your sense of deserving, or someone comes along and robs you of your Self-worth, it feels like it was lost to outside of you, and that is where you will go to look for it. You will work hard to gain acknowledgment or get recognized, you become a Bully, descend like a Vampire on those who still feel safe and drain them in an instant of what you need to fill your own hole by pretending that you are stronger, more powerful, and in control.

By the time we are grown up, our emotional body has so many holes, it looks like Swiss cheese.

The emotional body constantly reminds the unconscious Self to fill the empty spots. You are prompted and prodded by the unconscious Self to get rid of the pain caused by losing parts of who you really are. As you search outside your Self, none of what you find seems to stick for very long. The holes in your emotional body are bottomless pits and discard what comes from outside of Self quickly and mercilessly. Just like your physical body rejects foreign parts, the emotional body dismisses replacements that are alien to its own vibration.

While you have holes in your emotional body, you project from your Self the emotions that have taken residence in the absence of light. If you feel unworthy, you will behave as if you are unworthy, and start to believe that you are unworthy, due to the reality that is created by you feeling unworthy in the first place. It's a vicious cycle that can only be stopped by you.

Ask your Self if you have experienced feeling unworthy long enough to know what it means to be worthy? Did you even know what it meant to be worthy before you lost feeling worthy to someone who stole it from you? They could have done this with a simple hurtful remark and gotten away with your sense of worth before you even knew what happened. Well, it's time to replenish and refresh your emotional body by returning worth from within.

Filling your holes from within is the only way to restore your emotional body to its original glory.

Remind your Self of your worth by creating a list of everything that is great about you. List your talents, strengths, abilities and gifts. Remember that you are a precious child of the Universe, a magnificent Being of Light and love. Shed your veils and listen to your Heart voice instead of the one based on fear. Start to act as if you know you are worthy, behave in ways that support this notion, and before you know it, you will feel as if you are worthy. And as your reality begins to reflect it, your beliefs adjust, and once again you trust that you are worthy.

Feeling worthy is going to fill you with an amazing amount of joy. You are completely aware and mindful of its power, and recognize that you would never have truly understood what it means to be worthy unless you had lost it first. You have the power to reclaim each and every part of your emotional body by giving it back to your Self. And you will learn that it is your choice if you give your worth away again or not.

When you have worth, those who don't have it are hunting for it and might try to take it away from you. It is within your power to see this coming and to recognize it for what it really is. Someone taking your worth has nothing to do with you being unworthy and everything to do with them desperately looking for a way to fill their own hole. Their hole was created by someone else having stolen their worth. They rob from us because they've been robbed from. You get the picture.

How you respond to a Vampire is crucial. Have empathy for him. Take his energetic hooks out of your own emotional body and connect them back to the perpetrator's own Highest Source connection above his head between the seventh and eight chakras. A simple visualization is all it takes. Just imagine detaching the hook and placing it back where it belongs.

Stay calm and confident. Remind your Self that your opponent is hungry for what he lost, and give him what he needs through communication. Take a moment to get in touch with what you feel the hunter needs. Then acknowledge the need with empathy and sincerity.

If your boss, for example, is attempting to make you feel guilty for leaving work on time while she has to stay to finish something, she is looking to be acknowledged for how much she works, and often feels that all her dedication has gone unnoticed or is not appreciated. So instead of getting defensive or angry with your boss, give her what she needs. Let her know that you have noticed how much effort and dedication obviously goes into being in charge of a company, and how much you appreciate having a superior who is willing to stay longer to ensure that her employees can pick up their children from day care on time. Make sure you really mean what you say in order to avoid cynicism.

How many people are hooked into your battery -- the reservoir where you store the energy you need to feel vital and alive? And why are you allowing them to suck you dry? What are you getting from being emptied, used and drained? Ask your Self if being the Victim, the Martyr or the Good Samaritan are roles that provide you with some of what fills your holes from outside your Self, and decide to stop this destructive cycle.

Remove all the plugs you have firmly planted into the batteries of your loved ones, friends, and even strangers along the way. Become aware of what you are stealing away from others the very next time you notice that your demands are unreasonable, out of proportion, or placed solely to be in control. Are you furious that others are carefree while you are completely overworked? Give responsibility back to where it belongs, give up what weighs heavy on you because you took it on only to gain status, and gift your Self the delicious freedom of moments of carefreeness and playful abandon.

Those who have lost all the qualities of a little child still connected to Highest Source, who shines with purity, is completely innocent, fiercely protected, deliciously nurtured, and with the freedom of carefreeness intact, are the ones who will seek and destroy such a precious Being. It provides them with the food that temporarily fills the holes in their emotional body. Our prisons are filled with those who don't know how to restore their own emotional holes.

Imagine a world in which each person knows how to replenish the empty spaces in their emotional body and be one of the first ones to be whole!

Opus Lux Action Tip

The only thing you can control is how you respond to whatever is presented to you. Once you become aware that you do not have to allow others to take even the smallest piece out of your emotional body, you are on the way to recovery. Be mindful how you get your emotional holes filled. Say good-bye to feeling like Swiss cheese and hello to awesome wholeness!

~ The Power of Words ~

"Words have the power to both destroy and heal –
when words are both true and kind, they can change our world."
~Buddha~

The Universe we live in reacts to everything we feel, think, or say. Infinite possibilities are developed by what we project and emanate, and it is this outflow that creates the inflow of what we attract to ourselves. Entering into the world of duality, you get to experience the absence of light, and therefore are able to gain insight and acquaint your Self with contrasting concepts. Lack, disease, war, pain, struggle, loss, and everything else you might perceive as negative or dark, may have a devastating effect on you. The dark side of duality may produce feelings of powerlessness, or give you a sense of being out of control over what is happening all around you.

Have you noticed how much attention is given to all that we don't like? Everyone is complaining about everything, and nothing seems to work anymore.

We discuss what bothers, annoys, or makes us angry at length and in great detail. We watch others talk about the horrors of the world on TV and are bombarded with campaign slogans like "War on terrorism" or "Fight the battle against breast cancer," and then we're surprised that these issues have grown in unequaled proportions.

Words are infinitely more powerful than we realize. A single remark like "You look fat," "I hate your freckles," or "You are lazy," heard in childhood or before the target is mature enough to not take such an insult personally, can have a lasting effect. Life-long struggles can ensue. Declarations of anything that makes someone faulty, wrong or bad can eventually cause depression, body dysmorphia, cancer, and even claim lives.

Those who are aggressive with their words and actions are that way because nothing else has worked and that's the only way they will be heard and noticed. Others avoid confronting conflict, hold back how they really feel, thinking that this approach is going to create the peace they crave, and out of fear that they will be judged and consequently abandoned should they dare to express their true viewpoint or opinion. After all, we are here to experience opposites and then bring them into balance.

Balance is restored when the aggressive one becomes a little more like the nonconfrontational one, and the one who avoids conflict takes a slice off the loud and demanding one. Each of them being assertive in a respectful manner and on their own behalf as they pursue their own goals is consequently what creates the desired results.

"I confront conflict by communicating my needs and desires in an honest and loving way, staying calm and firm."

Miscommunication, failure to really listen, hearing what we would like to hear instead of what is being said, saying something that is incongruent just to please others or to make a desired impression, any form of gossip, downright lying, manipulation for gain, only talking about unimportant matters, defending to stay in control, failing to give clear instructions, lack of empathy, or using an irritated tone of voice, bold cynicism, being forbidden to communicate problems or secrets, are all forms of expression designed to feed the ever-widening gap between people, and all stem from acting on the whims and fancies of the Ego. With that said, examine your own communication patterns. Would you care what others thought or said about you if you knew that they were only doing so because they, themselves, were worried about fitting in, filling the holes in their emotional bodies by stealing your confidence, your authority, and your priceless Self-esteem? Are you policing others, making them wrong or bad, just to prove that you are better educated, more sophisticated, farther advanced, and have a higher status?

We have fallen for the dirty tricks of our Ego voice long enough. Are you ready to listen to your Heart voice and communicate in a congruent, direct, confident, and loving way? Communicating with your Self and others from the Heart instead of the Head opens the doors to a peaceful world. Say only what you truly mean, and walk your talk. Do your best to understand why or how others are interestingly different from you. Discern what works for you and what doesn't, and learn to agree to disagree.

Acknowledge others' wounds with empathy and really listen to what they are saying. There is no need to take the blame or feel responsible for what they feel. Respond by saying, "That must have been so painful for you," or "You must be really tired after all you've gone through in the past couple of weeks." Tune in to what they are feeling, and confirm what you hear, instead of saying something designed to make them feel "better," like "You are so much better off without him," or "Stop worrying, not everyone loses their hair from chemotherapy."

Slow down long enough to respond rather than react to what others are saying. Be deliberate and figure out what you would like to communicate with your response. You do not need to fix other people's problems! Women especially are often just looking for a sounding board. Say, "I hear you," "That sounds very interesting," and "Yeah, hmm, aha," and other sounds that indicate that you are listening. Ask them, "What are you going to do about this?" or say, "I know you will find an answer to this issue," or "I have complete faith in your ability to solve this challenge."

This supports the notion that you believe in them and gives them a boost in Self-reliance.

Even if you see the bigger picture and know exactly what others need to change to better their situation, lead them to their own answer by asking them how they are planning to solve their problem. Ask questions like, "Have you thought about how this will affect you, your son, your job, your relationship?" or "What is the best solution you can think of right now?" Men tend to figure things out on their own, and when they ask you for a solution, they are genuinely interested in your opinion. Ask, "Are you looking for a different viewpoint or my opinion?" before venturing into fix-it mode. When someone is asking for your viewpoint or opinion on a particular issue, tell them an example out of your own experience that dealt with a similar situation and ended with a desirable result.

~

Being blamed about something that you don't feel responsible for can trigger aggression, lead you to defend your Self, and can easily end up in discord, disconnection, or a big fight. Respond instead of reacting, stay confident, and say, "I'm sorry you feel this way," or "I realize there is a misunderstanding. This is what I really meant to say" -- which leads to the importance of asking for feedback when we communicate our ideas, viewpoints, or opinions to others.

After communicating an important idea, after giving instructions, or after clarifying a miscommunication, always ask for feedback. Say, "Would you please tell me what you heard me say, so I can be sure I was heard?" This helps to minimize misunderstandings and leaves no room for assumptions. Everyone has buttons that can be pushed by how we say something or by what we communicate to them. For a person who was told they are fat, a simple statement like "You sure seem hungry today" can rip the scab right off the old wound, create resentment, and open the floodgate to sometimes ancient, buried emotional pain. You, on the other hand, were looking for a compliment on your great meal and got an icy stare instead. It is your choice to give away your confidence and become insecure, or to remember that when others get triggered by what you say, it's about them, not about you.

~

Discussing problems is dreaded by most humans because they may start to feel like they are being attacked, blamed, and believe they are seen as bad, wrong, or indifferent. It makes a big difference when you approach large contrasts in viewpoint or opinion by asking the other person for an appointment, a time set apart when both parties have time and are prepared to respond to what is put on the table. Ask, "When would be a good time for you to talk about this issue?" and "I think that it will take about an hour."

Bringing the topic up at an inconvenient time or out of context can create stress and impatience. Complaining, nagging, and constantly bringing up an ongoing problem will erode the strongest foundation in any relationship. You may get a "yes" from the other person just to get you off their back, and will end up being disappointed or disillusioned when they conveniently "forget" or deny ever having made a promise or a commitment.

Set an appointed time and give each participant a turn to be heard. Put all ideas, viewpoints, and opinions on the table, and aim to create a win-win situation. No one has to lose, no one has to compromise, and everyone is open to finding a solution that is even better than what each one of you has proposed. Creating a win-win solution requires cooperation. You are looking for a third solution that is above and beyond the initial ideas and sometimes depends on help from a mediator or the use of a talking stick that you pass around until all are heard. Be on time, and schedule another appointment if you are still negotiating. Negotiate what is fair and create an equal energy exchange. As you voice your ideas, complaints, viewpoints, and opinions, make the statements about you. "I would love to spend more quality time with you" assures a much better outcome than "You never have time for me because work is obviously more important to you." Using "you" will sound like an attack and lead to a defensive reaction rather than an opening to an amicable conversation.

State what you would like instead of what no longer works for you. Say, "I could use your help right now. Would you be willing to vacuum the living room before our guests get here?" instead of "You never help, and I always end up doing everything my Self!" Get together with your family or roommates and negotiate house rules. Devise a plan for chores or anything else that causes quarrels in your immediate environment. Include everyone that is affected or is part of the issue at hand, negotiate a fair agreement, and follow through with the conditions and consequences to which all committed.

Treat each and every one of your family members like a guest you have great reverence for. Include your Self in this approach. You are a Light-Being having a physical experience, and even though you are heavily veiled and often forget that you and everyone else is filled with Creator energy, apologize to your Self and others when you wake up after a spell of confusion about who you or they are and step back into a state of grace.

When you have reverence for your Self and all other sentient Beings you come in contact with, you will no longer tolerate being treated with disrespect, and you'll express your personal boundaries in an honest and loving way, staying calm and firm. You will recognize when others have forgotten their true nature, and communicate in a new way, allowing them to go through what they are here to experience without taking it personally or feeling blamed.

How would you ask your husband to do something for you if he was your favorite actor? What if your daughter was the person you admired most growing up? Would you be impatient with the clerk at your grocery store if he was a high-standing, adored leader of your community? Would you be mean to your Self if you were your best friend?

~

By choosing powerful words, you communicate to your best advantage. Here are a few examples of do's and don'ts:

Don't:

The Universe does NOT understand the word NOT
(The Universe does ___ understand the word ___)
Every time you think or talk about something that you do NOT want anymore, you produce more of it.
A want is a lack, and the Universe will do everything in its power to correct this. Whenever you want something, you will lack it.
Example: I don't want to be poor (I do___ lack to be poor)
This also explains why children do what you ask them not to do. "Don't run across the street without looking!"

Do:

State what you would like or DESIRE instead! The word desire means: "Of God." Completely eliminate the word "want" from your vocabulary!
Example: I desire to be abundant.
Communicate to your child what you would like them to do, and be dazzled by how much more willing they are to comply. "Stop and look to your left and to your right to make sure it's safe to cross the street."

Don't:

When you EXPECT something, you are going to have to wait and wait for whatever you are expecting to show up in your life.
The dictionary lists: "Expectant: Waiting for something to happen."

Do:

INTEND and feel as if you already have what you desire.
The dictionary lists: "Intended: meant or planned."

Don't:

In many instances, the word BUT negates everything you just said.
Example: "I'm sending an application to the college I would love to attend, but think that my grades are not good enough.

Do:
Use the word AND instead.
Example: "I'm sending an application to the college I would love to attend and intend that my grades are good enough."

Don't:
The word TRY is a halfhearted attempt. There is no try. Either you do you don't. When someone has tried to do something, it indicates that the attempt was unsuccessful. The following statement sounds insincere.
Example: "I tried to call you."
Do:
Simply apologize.
Example: "I apologize for failing to call you. "Will you please forgive me?"

Don't:
HOPE is something that leaves us powerless, something that we have no control over. We hope that something will occur to help us....
Do:
FAITH is an inner knowing a belief that leaves us in charge and gives us the power to manifest anything we feel is possible.

Don't:
Sometimes we get angry with another person and we express our frustration in the following way: "YOU ALWAYS forget to bring out the trash and YOU NEVER help me!"
Do:
It is very important to share our feelings, good or bad. It is equally important to make the challenge your own issue and take full responsibility for how it makes you feel. Say, "I feel overwhelmed with the household. I am tired and would appreciate your help."

Don't:
KIND OF, SORT OF are wishy-washy terms that are very vague. They are similar to the word "try." Either you do or you don't.
Example: "I sort of, kind of, tried to have no expectations, but failed."
The above example sounds like you hardly put any effort into succeeding, and gives the impression that you are giving up.
Do:
Be clear what you communicate. Make up your mind on how

something really affected you and how much you truly desire to change.
Example: "I'm doing my best to lay down all expectations, and it is challenging."
The above example lets everyone know you are doing your best, and that you are taking on the challenge to change.

Don't:
A SHOULD is always something someone else would like you to do!
Example: "You should join a gym and eat healthier."
Do:
We resist being told what to do, even if it would be good for us. Only offer advice or recommendations to others when asked for your opinion. Otherwise, just be a shining example.
Example: "I have so much more energy since I've taken classes at the gym and started eating mostly organic and less processed foods."

Don't:
When you ask someone if they COULD do something for you, they will think, "Am I being asked if I'm capable of doing this task?" It is almost an insult to ask a grown man if he can take out the trash. Of course he CAN (in other words, he is capable of)! This may be the reason why the reaction to this nice sounding question is more often than not met with indignation and a refusal to comply.
Do:
Now ask the same man if he WOULD be willing to take out the trash, and you will get a completely different reaction. When you ask it in this way, you give the person a choice to say yes or no. Once committed to a yes, it is an agreement and much more likely to be kept, since most humans have a desire to live up to their promises. If the answer is no, it may be time to negotiate a fair chore list with deadlines and appropriate consequences.

Don't:
Being told what to do by others creates resistance and we tend to just dismiss what they are saying. Confusing the voice in our head with the voice in our heart can limit us in a similar way.
Do:
Discern between your louder Ego voice and your smaller, stiller Heart voice and truly listen to what sounds true from within as well as from outside your Self. Learn to follow and trust your true inner voice and discern what resonates with you that comes from outside

your Self - which is essential for your decision-making power and personal individual expression.

Don't:
Don't sell out! Making an exception that compromises your personal or professional boundaries to please someone you care about or feel obligated towards is socially expected and is widely used as a bargaining technique.
Do:
Negotiate within your established boundaries and freely communicate the fact that you treat everyone the same. When you keep your integrity intact you gain respect, transmit trust and project, "I deserve to be honored."

Don't:
Do you just walk away or give unmistakable signs of impatience with your body language to end a conversation?
Do:
A closing statement like "I really enjoyed talking with you," "Here is my business card, please contact me if you have any further questions" or "I wish I could stay longer and need to speak with.... before I leave," in combination with a friendly handshake is effective and courteous.

Don't:
Today's technology allows us to communicate per text, e-mail or on social networking sites like facebook or twitter. It's easy to share bad news or complaints in this way because we don't have to face the person directly and are at a safe distance when they receive the message.
Do:
Be courageous and only text that you would like to talk in private and ask for a face-to-face meeting when you plan to communicate anything negative, important or of intimate nature. If you fear a negative response, meet in a neutral place that allows for privacy, yet is public enough to keep the person receiving any bad or upsetting news from lashing out.

Don't:
If you are the boss and need to address a problem with an employee, you may not realize what kind of effect the stress of the situation has on the one of your voice. You could come across as harsh, unreasonable

or indifferent and this can create resistance, resentment or contempt in the people you count on.

Do:

Take a step back to assess the situation before you address your staff. Decide what you would like to accomplish with what you communicate, and then confront the conflict in the same manner you would like to be addressed, if the roles were reversed. Keep the tone of your voice calm and what you say factual. Your team-members will learn that they can trust your ability to stay composed, collected and will settle at the eye of the hurricane, instead of getting swept up and carried away.

Don't:

Don't tell your co-workers how unfair it is that you didn't get a raise or were not considered for a position you would have loved to have.

Do:

Tell your boss! When you know exactly what you desire, have considered why you deserve a raise or what makes you the best possible choice to fill a particular position in the company you work for, make an appointment with your higher-up and ask for what you would like. Clarity about your intentions and the confidence to ask for what you desire communicates your direction and ambitions. Should you be denied, ask what you can do differently to achieve your goals.

Don't:

Someone who uses "I" more than "You" may wonder why they have such a hard time connecting to others.

Do:

When you desire to create a deeper connection to others pay attention and use "You" as much as you use "I."

Tell others how you would like to be supported!

You know what you need and would be surprised to find that your loved ones are much more eager to please than you think. To be of help to others is a deep desire anchored within human nature. You help others with what you feel or think they need without them asking because that's how you would like to be helped if it were the other way around. Each of us has a good idea of what we need from others but are afraid to ask because we are worried that we might come across as ungrateful or spoiled. Did you notice that the word "but" in the last sentence overrode what we innately know is for our Highest Good? Instead of "Yes, but," say, "Why not?"

Example: "I so appreciate your desire to assist me with my hospital stay, and here is what will support me most. I feel nervous about having anyone other than my boyfriend in the room with me right after I have my surgery and would appreciate it if everyone else stayed home and prayed for me. This will help me to focus on my Self instead of being concerned about how everyone else is doing, yet still know that I am in your thoughts and hearts. Thank you for being so considerate. I love you all."

Heart-based communication has the power to heal your Self, your relationships, and is an essential element of what we attract to ourselves and what kind of reality we manifest. Listening to your heart and expressing your ideas, viewpoints, and opinions shows your willingness to take the risk to be judged and consequently abandoned. Your cellular memory remembers past lives. Only fifty years ago, those who spoke from their heart, or shared knowledge derived from Higher Source, were silenced, burned at the stake, imprisoned, or tarred and feathered.

Is this why you are holding back? Ask your Self, "What is the worst that could happen," and understand that we live in a place on Mother Earth where freedom of speech is only interrupted by those who at worst incinerate or defile you with hateful words. It is your choice to give them your power or to remain confident in your own integrity and your own truth. Allow them to be interestingly different, do your best to understand why they see the world with different eyes, accept them without having to agree, and go where you are invited.

Opus Lux Action Tip

For at least two weeks, each morning remind your Self of the power of communication. Say to your Self, "At first, it is most important that I express my own viewpoint at all. Once I become comfortable in voicing my opinion, I start to pay attention to how I communicate and begin to refine my skills. I stay away from those who gossip, complain without looking for a solution, listen to my own inner guidance, and follow my own advice."

~ 12 Commonly Believed Lies ~

"Believe nothing, no matter where you read it or who said it,
no matter if I have said it, unless it agrees with
your own reason and your own common sense."
~Buddha~

Here are a few examples of belief patterns that have turned out to be lies. Examine your own beliefs in order to excavate and let go of those which no longer serve you. Slow down for a moment and ask your heart if your own belief systems handed down from generation to generation really feel true. Replace them with fresh new insights and create belief patterns that reflect your innate truth and line up with your personal integrity.

1. It is selfish to take care of my Self first.
2. What I give to others or do for others will come back to me tenfold.
3. If I am stronger than the other person, I have to help them carry their load.
4. I am responsible for my Mother, Father, Husband, Wife, Coworker, etc.
5. Random events that I have no control over can happen to me at any time.
6. Being a people pleaser shows that I am a considerate, kind person.
7. The harder I push, the stronger I get.
8. I am responsible for other people's happiness.
9. If I am true to my Self, I will be judged and consequently abandoned.
10. To forgive others I have to be okay with what they did.
11. I have to rely on others to fill my needs, and they can depend on me.
12. Keep doing what you are doing, and if you persist long enough, you will succeed.

Opus Lux Action Tip

Make your own list of beliefs or perspectives that no longer serve you and replace them with new insights you feel good about.

~ Manifestation ~

"It is our light, not our darkness, that most frightens us."
~Nelson Mandela~

The secret to manifesting your desires with ease and grace is very simple. The ability to move beyond the limitations of the Magician is at your fingertips. You are now ready to leave behind you the archetype of the one who was out of alignment with his inner knowing and created the illusion of success by working hard to manifest false ideas or dreams into reality. It's the Wizard who magically, and seemingly out of nowhere, magnetizes all resources necessary to fulfill his dreams, and he is the one who creates the desired reality effortlessly and with ease and grace.

The glaring difference between the Magician and the Wizard is that the first relies entirely on logic and the Male attributes of hard work, status, and success based on material gain. The other connects the Mind with the Heart, aims to live his true purpose, and builds his success on doing what he loves and being who he is.

Glorious results come from deliberate actions that are taken based on the degree they serve the fulfillment of our life's purpose. Define your highest vision of your Self, decide to go into the direction of your dreams, design an action plan, and do what is possible today, within your current means, and this is what gets you closer to your desired outcome. The imagined outcome is like a carrot dangling on a stick, drawing you along your path, but may not necessarily be where you find your Self at the end of your journey.

Along the way, you might come to a fork in the road and choose a new direction that you would never have found had you not followed the metaphorical carrot. If something looks even better than the initially desired outcome, change your vision. It's all part of the mystery! How boring life would be if we knew exactly what was going to happen next.

You know you are on your path and are lined up with your purpose when everything flows. As soon as you find your Self pushing too hard for a specific outcome or forcing an issue, you are no longer lined up with your true mission.

Stop right there and take some time to reflect.

Have you been taught that if you persist and hold on long enough, you will eventually get the desired result? "Don't give up," they said. "Keep doing what you are doing. It's just a matter of will, a test of your strength, an assessment to see if you have what it takes to succeed." What they didn't tell you, is, that it is not by repeating the same action again and again that you eventually get the desired result. It is by changing the action, which then creates a different consequence that will eventually manifest the result you are after.

Each action has a specific predetermined consequence and a fixed result. Use your inner wisdom to foresee the consequences of your actions to create the desired result.

By gently changing your approach until you have found the action that creates the consequence that eventually manifests the desired result, you are guaranteed to be victorious.

Repeating the same action to create a different result is called insanity.

Experience and observation of cause and effect leads to wisdom. One aspect of wisdom is to tap into the reservoir of your own life experiences and gathered knowledge to foresee the consequences of your actions. Being immersed in duality allows you to compare, analyze, and see the contrast and the difference. Then choose what works for you. We start as the Fool and end as the Sage.

~

Now that you've defined your direction, are doing what is possible to do within your current means, are following your "carrot," are going with the flow, are using your inner wisdom to foresee the consequences of your actions, and are willingly adjusting your actions, you are given everything you need to accomplish your goal. All the resources you may need, people with special talents that complement your purpose, the investor, a bank loan, an inheritance, or anything else you may feel or think you need to accomplish your goal, will usually show up exactly when you need them and not a second sooner.

Don't sit and wait for something you don't need at this very moment! Complete the tasks at hand that you can do right now without the perceived necessity. Keep the job that sustains your basic needs until your true purpose supplies what you need. Grow your dream organically, one step after another. A good foundation needs to be solid. Everything you have done in your life has sharpened your talents, added strength, and deepened your gifts.

Do you feel that others are luckier than you and seemingly without effort attract what they need to live the life of their dreams? Guess what? Luck is merely a combination of preparation, sharpening your skills, and taking opportunities when they come—not something those more fortunate have had placed in their crib by a fairy godmother. The more you prepare your Self, hone your skills, and take the opportunities as they arrive, the luckier you will be.

~

Becoming a Wizard requires practice and trust. Keep following your Heart's promptings. Use your logic to come up with a plan that creates great results with the least effort, and make the needed adjustments as you go. Get excited about each accomplishment, and celebrate even the smallest achievements. You instantly move to the next level of your personal evolution the moment you are content with what is right now. Struggle, fear, and high expectations are the greatest enemies of the budding Wizard, so keep your vibration high and your thoughts positive.

Life is not a fairy tale. You will not be rescued, swept off your feet, and live happily ever after. Life is an adventure, a place where you walk around with a blindfold and have to figure out the difference between who you are and who you are not. Each of us is part of the whole, and as a whole we are everything that is, was, or will be. In the illusion of separateness you get to define what you are passionate about and learn to trust that you have a perfectly designed Higher Plan. Everything is always in Divine order, and you are drawing to your Self exactly what you need right here and now.

~

Use powerful words when you proclaim what you intend to manifest. Focus on what you would like to create, and ask for what you feel is possible right now. How you treat your Self is what creates how you feel, and how you feel is what you project from you, and this is what will come back to you! Outflow creates inflow. What you choose is what you will be given more of. Be careful to make choices that are aligned with what you desire to manifest in your life.

If you are looking for a committed romantic relationship, don't choose someone who will take you out on dates but shows no sign of settling down with one particular person. It's as if your Higher Self looks down on you to see what you are choosing in order to bring you more of the same. Your Higher Self is eager to please, and does not discern if something fits your idea of what should be. It simply brings you more of what you choose.

~

Example: A personal observation regarding manifestation on the home front.

Even though my husband, Tim, and I have lived together for a long time, I buy my own groceries and will only eat some of the things he cooks. He has always thought it was the strangest thing that I don't like the kind of pizza that is delivered from one of the local fast-food places, or would turn down his generous offering of preparing hotdogs on a white bun. Tim has a true sweet-tooth and a love for desserts. Haagen Dazs rum-raison ice cream is one of his favorites. Oreo cookies with a tall glass of cold milk an easy runner-up.

In the beginning of our relationship, I would ask if he really needed two candy bars for a visit to the movie theater, or another serving of high-carbohydrate foods like mashed potatoes, and freely commented on the highly-processed food choices he often made. My interference was met with resistance, so I started to back off. I watched, I waited, and was the best example I could be.

One day Tim came home from a doctor visit and told me that he had high blood sugar. He bought the book his doctor had recommended. The title was "Sugar Busters," and it remained unread on the nightstand next to his bed. A few months later he shared the devastating news that he was diagnosed with type 2 diabetes. I was not surprised at all, which greatly irritated him. He started to exercise more, lost some weight, and made healthier food choices. And then he returned to eating like he used to, got some medication to keep things in check, and lost interest in cardiovascular exercise.

Not long ago, we had invited friends for dinner, and Tim was supposed to be home at six o'clock. Instead he called to inform me that he was at the local Med-Stop seeing a doctor. He had felt dizzy, was strangely disoriented, and had a really high blood sugar reading. Motivated by this scare, he again sought help. He works for Hospice, and one of the nutritionists at work helped him put a new diet plan into action. Interestingly to me, this plan included lots of carbohydrates (which turn into sugar), processed canned fruit, and more peanut-butter than your typical first-grader consumes.

Tim was really upset with the fact that he had not paid enough attention to his diet or had not been more assertive with his exercise plan. The nutritionist assured him that there was nothing he could have done differently in the past, and that diabetes is a condition that can be treated with medication. The blood sugar readings remained high, and the nutritionist recommended that he seek a doctor who would be willing to prescribe insulin, a commercial preparation of polypeptide hormones that are normally produced by the pancreas. She was concerned about his vision and other damage that can occur in the physical body when the blood sugar is high, and something needed to be done.

I made some comments that went unheard, and then I watched and waited. My husband's doctor recommended that he build muscle mass and eat better, and gave him a sample insulin pen to take home. Tim was confused and afraid to make the wrong choice. He finally asked me for my opinion and was ready to look at the metaphysical reason that caused him to behave the way he had.

It was as if he was sitting on a fence. On one side, he could live life to the fullest, not worry about whatever he ate or how much he exercised, take insulin to cover up the deficiency, and die a miserable early death. On the other side was what appeared to be a much harder course. He would have to spend energy figuring out a diet that would keep his blood sugar low, add cardiovascular training and muscle-building exercises, and slowly wean him Self off the medication he was already taking. In return, he would feel more vital, have more energy, and, more likely, live a healthy long life.

Tim decided to get his health back and undo what years of bad habits had caused. To my surprise, he even made an appointment with an acupuncturist who came recommended by one of his friends. On the way home he called me and said that she'd told him that there are no acupuncture treatments to help with diabetes. She prescribed herbs and explained that insulin was a very good choice to treat his condition. I laughed and thought he was just joking with me. No acupuncture? How funny! Well, it turned out he wasn't kidding at all. Just like the type of nutritionist he had energetically attracted, he had found one of the few acupuncturists that were lined up with his previous way of being. You get more of what you choose!

It was certainly interesting to observe that the Western Medical Doctor encouraged Tim to get off the drugs while the Nutritionist and the Doctor of Acupuncture steered him in the direction of taking insulin. And with that, he would simply be covering up the bad behaviors. As a little side note, once you change direction, make sure you surround your Self with those who will support your new choice! There is no right or wrong. Either choice has value. They are just interestingly different, and will lead to contrasting results. Tim could have chosen to go either way. It was up to him. It's his life, and he gets to make choices and decisions that please and serve him, while I get to make choices and decisions that please and serve me.

For years, I had been tempted to interfere with Tim's choices. It was like I was sitting there, watching him make one less than healthy decision after another, without saying anything. The funny thing is that, while all the above was going on, he had driven into town and parked in a parking space where he had to feed a meter with change. As he was inserting enough money for an hour, a parking lot patrol cart stopped right next to his car. The female attendant just sat there and watched him. When he came back twenty minutes later, he found a ticket under his windshield wiper. He had fed the meter on the right instead of the one on the left, and the woman had watched him make the mistake without saying anything. Man, was he angry.

I thought it was a perfect sign. For a long time, his own inner Male had not considered the inner Female and her promptings to do what truly felt right to him. I'm not sure he could have heard any woman outside of him Self as long as he could not hear the one inside. When he finally combined the Mind with the Heart, Tim found it much easier to make the choices and decisions that serve him best. It made me very happy that my husband was now manifesting a foundation for a long and happy life. I was thrilled that he was able to slow down long enough to hear his Heart voice and follow it. And last, but not least, with the path he is now on, we are going to be climbing mountaintops instead of spending time in a hospital dealing with the sometimes severe consequences of diabetes. Yea!

Tim deserves a humongous "thank you" for his amazing courage to allow me to share with you his most vulnerable side in such a public way. When I first asked him if I could share his story, he had no idea how he would feel after the initial read-through. Needless to say, he felt criticized and exposed. My heart went out to him. Yet still, I asked, if just one person is spared from a similar fate, would it be worth it? There are millions of people who make lifestyle choices with detrimental consequences, and because so many others live the same way, they all think they will be okay. Breaking the taboo sure wasn't easy!

~

Follow your Ego voice and you will get an experience that shows you who you are not – follow your Heart voice and you will get an experience that shows you who you truly are.

If you always do for others, and fail to do for your Self, your Higher Self will send you more opportunities where you will be expected to do more for others than your Self. Should you wish for extra money, don't spend everything you have, like you may have done all your life. Keep some, and more to keep is sure to follow. Are you constantly talking about lack, feel like there is never enough, or that nothing will ever change, and continually surprised that you get more of the same, even though you asked the Universe to send you relief?

To bring more abundance into your existence, be grateful for what you already have. Look around and notice that 99% of the world is a balanced cornucopia of bountiful beauty. Stop waiting to be rescued and fill your own cup until it overflows. This will allow you to be more generous with your Self, and your Higher Self can finally bring you the opportunities you've been asking for.

Highly effective decision-making process:

Each action has a set consequence and a predetermined result. Actions that lead to what we call "mistakes" are feared and are often responsible for inaction or indecision. The more mistakes we make, the wiser we become. Eventually we will be familiar with the cause and effect of many of our actions. The ability to foresee the consequences of one's actions is the mark of the Wise Sage. Often we fall into the trap of the Ego, labor as hard as the Magician, and only create the illusion of a successful outcome. Below is a practical recipe to activate your inner Wizard.

The pineal gland, which is located at the center of your brain, looks like a small pine cone on a stem and works like a television set. When turned on, it ensures reception of Higher Knowing. You get a visual effect of the information through images seen with the third eye and hear its sound with your inner voice. To access the best reception, ask to be connected to Highest Good, Highest Truth, and Highest Source possible. Your crown chakra needs to be open to receive information from your subconscious. The subconscious is the all-knowing Creator energy that broadcasts the extrasensory images and internal sound effects you perceive as dreams, visions, and the brilliant ideas you are blessed with when you are tuned in. The more you trust your extrasensory perception, the more you use your imagination, the more you meditate, the clearer your connection to Higher Knowing.

Follow these easy steps to reach decisions that are for your Highest Good and lead to actions that create consequences and results you will love.

1. Ask to be connected to information for your Highest Good, Highest Truth, and from Highest Source.
2. Turn on your internal TV, meditate, daydream, or slightly space out.
3. Think about the question you have for Highest Source. Ask to be shown the easiest, most graceful way to solve a problem, disentangle from an issue, or take the next step on your journey.
4. Ask for your sixth chakra to be activated and to be shown a picture of the highest vision or best idea. With your imagination/ third eye, look at your inner flat-screen.
5. If the picture you see looks great, exciting or desirable, send it down to the fifth chakra, in the area of your throat, and turn on the sound.
6. Here, you hear the sound of two different voices. First you become aware of the louder, fear-based Ego voice. It will give you all the reasons why what looks so great isn't going to work. It may tell you that you don't have the money or the time, that your family is not going to approve, and that you should just forget about it. Remember that the Ego does not like change, and send it to the sideline. Tune into your Heart and ask your Heart voice if what the Ego voice is saying is really true. Your Heart

voice is based on trust and will give you all the reasons why what looks so good is achievable and perfect for you. It may not be "normal" or "rational," but it is definitely the next natural step to take, and very much part of your path.

7. Once you have found your true message, shift your focus to your Heart space, located in your fourth chakra, and check in with your feelings to determine if what looks so great and sounds so natural also feels exciting. There has to be at least some measure of joy, enthusiasm or sense of adventure for you to know that you are about to make a good choice. If there is no joy, if your Heart does not say, "Yes, yes, yes," don't choose it! Before you come to any important decisions, always say, "Ladies first." This means that the first factor in the decision-making process is based on the qualities of your inner Female, and her voice is represented by the internal Heart voice. The degree of her enthusiasm is the gauge on how well this decision is going to serve you.
8. As soon as you feel the joy in your heart, the next door opens to give access to the wisdom of the third chakra, which is located in the area of your solar plexus. Here you ask, "Will what looks so amazing and sounds so right empower me?" You, not anyone else. So don't listen to the Ego voice that has become bored standing on the sideline and has snuck down to the second chakra to activate new triggers. "What about those you are responsible for? What will happen to them if you fail? What will others think or say?" Here is where a good many plans are aborted, left behind, and dismissed as Self-indulgent fantasies. Never send your vision to the traps of the second chakra!
9. If your vision, your dream, your idea empowers you, go for it! If it empowers you, everyone affected by your decision will benefit in an as of now possibly unforeseen manner. At this point you need to call in your inner Male to create an action plan. The inner Female sits together with the inner Male until the best possible plan has been designed. He uses his logic, his rationale, and his common sense. He does the math and analyzes how the pieces fit together while she constantly questions if his choices are going to create the best results with the least effort. It's her job to ensure that the action plan can be done with ease and grace. Flow is key. Force is a red flag and will cause only strife.
10. The inner Male is the one who takes the action steps to bring the vision, the dream, the idea into physical manifestation. He consults with the inner Female as he runs into unforeseen blocks or obstacles on the road whenever he finds him Self forcing or

pushing, and together they create magical results.

11. The changes may initially cause disruption or create a void, and this may fuel your Ego voice. Eventually your new actions will fill the emptiness with what finally sustains you. Your particular purpose for this life may have many facets. It could take you a long time to accumulate all the knowledge required to live it. A good sign that you are still sharpening your skills is the state of Being in which you have not been able to create an overflow of abundance. Instead, all you ever seem to experience is just getting by. If you have not been wildly successful yet, then you are still gathering the tools or skills necessary to live your true life's purpose. Keep changing your actions ever so slightly until you create the desired result. Experiment, to see how close you can get to the highest vision of your Self. Remember, there is no need to prove anything. Just experiment.
12. Everything you have experienced, learned and encountered in your life so far has provided an important element of your true life's mission. Move forward to the next level when your Heart desires change. Give up what no longer serves you to make room for the new. Know that if you have not managed to be greatly successful with your last effort to create abundance, you may have settled or are not yet evolved to the point where you can really live your life's true calling. Combine the wisdom of your Heart with the logic of your Mind. Create synergy and equal energy between your inner Male and your inner Female. This speeds up the process, eliminates staying in a situation too long or not long enough, and before you know it, you have shed the skins of the hard-working Magician and fully stepped into the archetype of the Wizard.
13. You know you are a true Wizard when you embrace obstacles as an opportunity to grow. You are content with what is right now, and recognize that you have put each challenge on your own plate. Excitement fills you because your wisdom will be enhanced by understanding that solutions are available simply by turning on your inner television. You are now in the fast-lane and are getting closer and closer to your authentic Self.

~

Example: A personal account of transformation.

For many years I worked for minimal compensation or for free. First for my mom in her flower shop, then for my boss in my four-year display artist apprenticeship, and another thirteen years for my first husband in his travel service and rental fleet for Swiss tourists business. Helping others succeed with their goals had been underscored and was driven by the concept and belief that what you do for others will come back to you tenfold, which turned out to be a lie.

Deep down I knew that being of service to others is truly what I desired to do with my life. What I failed to do was to include my Self in the equation and make my Self and my own well-Being as important as the welfare of others. My Self-worth had taken a big blow by the lack of proper compensation for my hard work. I continued to struggle with finances even after my divorce, when I was finally able to focus my energy towards my own goals.

I had such a desire to give to others what I never had and was generous with others even if I had nothing left for my Self. I would tell my Self that the little money I had needed to be spent on groceries the kids would like. I would eat whatever they did. When I bought them the clothes they needed, I told my Self that there wasn't enough left to get that nice blouse I had seen. At work, I gave those in financial straits a better deal than I could really afford. And when my office mates complained about a lack of clients, I would give them my share on top of theirs. Mind you, they did not expect me to do this. Nor did they ask. An inner compulsion to give to those who were in need held me like a puppet on a string. I never told anyone, and it was done only to make others feel better. Not to hunt for glory. My holes filled by seeing their relief. I was able to make them feel worthy and deserving by giving them what I didn't have growing up. But, as you now know, this euphoria didn't last for very long. Whenever there was a little extra, I spent it on something that was worn down from use, invited my friends for lunch, or bought an expensive gift for those I wished I could truly afford it for. My ability to pretend that I had plenty to give away became so polished in its execution that I almost believed I had this much to offer.

Always just barely making it took its toll. I had already grown up poor. Was I doomed to a life of scarcity, lack, and money worries? For years I wrote checks that were not yet covered, and miraculously the bare essentials showed up somehow and just in the nick of time. Had I not worked hard enough? Was I not deserving or worthy of the abundance others seemingly created with ease? I decided to take a closer look at what was missing in my recipe for financial success.

My dad had passed away when I was four years old. He had been our provider and our nurturer. My mom did her best to sustain us, but struggled to support us, which in turn created holes in my emotional body. Not having enough money to buy healthy food, decent clothes, or anything special while growing up, had left me feeling unworthy. The lack of nurturing had created a feeling that I was undeserving. I did everything in my power to make sure my loved ones would never feel this way!

Self-worth is closely tied to money and wealth. When you know and live your own worth, material abundance is a natural byproduct.

The men I picked were frugal in nature. They read the energy I projected, which announced in big letters, "She doesn't need anything. Give it all to others." Since I was ignoring my own needs and desires, I energetically projected from me, and thereby asked of them, to ignore my needs and desires. And here I was wondering why so little came my way! Unconsciously, I had selected those who were least prone to provide for me and nurture me in the way my father hadn't. I even got my Self into bankruptcy. The man in my life at that time could have helped me but didn't. I was devastated. Did he not love me? I asked my Higher Guidance and said:

Why is my partner unwilling to help me financially when I really need it? Does he not love me?

Imagine for a moment that he would have said, "How much do you need? I'll write you a check." What would this have felt like?

Wow, that would have been amazing. I would have felt such relief!

Now picture him saying, "And you never have to pay me back."

Even better! With all my worries gone, I would have a new start and could breathe again!

Would you have felt that you owed him?

Knowing me, yes. I would have been at his beck and call from here forth and for the rest of my life.

Is this really what you desire?

No. What I really would like is to just be able to provide for my Self, nurture my Self, and create an abundant life for my Self, without having to be at the mercy of someone outside of my Self.

~

Until that moment, I had never noticed that I had been waiting for the men in my life to prove to me that I deserved to be provided for and

nurtured. All of a sudden I could clearly see all the situations I had created to cause lack. I promised my Self that I would learn how to truly take care of my Self, fill each and every one of my needs, include my Self in the picture, create an abundant life, and be completely responsible for all of my actions. This meant that I needed to observe those who already had what I desired and copy them. Later I figured out that I also needed to become a bit more like those who I disliked.
After all, it benefited me to learn all I could about cause and effect and bring my own imbalances into harmony.

I started to divide our grocery and new clothing money fairly among all of us, including me. I raised my prices to the standard rate and no longer gave away free or discounted sessions. Just look at that word, "Discount." It says, "Discount what she does!" Learning to apply the 80/20 rule was hard. This rule is based on the concept that the initial 20% of our efforts creates 80% of the result. Some of us then use the remaining 80% of our energy to lift the last 20% to perfection. Quality is important, and an 80% result is usually enough to create the desired result. My inner Female started to remind my inner Male from time to time to use our energy wisely, and he then sent my inner Slave-Driver and his best friend, the inner Perfectionist, on a vacation.

If it wasn't mine, I gave back responsibility to whomever it belonged. This included allowing my own children to take full responsibility for their lives. And I feel very content knowing that, even though they struggle at times, they have wings that are fully feathered. There is nothing more amazing than watching them fly on their own. All they need is someone that completely believes in them. "Yes, you can. Don't you dare let anyone tell you that you can't!"

Using the decision-making process described above has allowed me to know when it was time to give up my massage practice and solely focus on providing energy healing and DNA reprogramming. It helped me to stay calm when the economy declined, and urged me to close my healing center and to stay in the house we rented rather than buying a house, as we had planned, after Tim and I got married. With less income and a lot more time on my hands, my Ego voice demanded that I get a job. Everyone else is doing it to survive! My Heart voice informed me that it was high time I learned to be content with what is and to write the book you are holding in your hands. It felt great to have used this time to share the secrets I have learned with you.

To this day, I still catch my Self giving away too much of my time. I sometimes buy excessive amounts of food when I have guests, or notice that I splurge on something special before I check my budget. Being aware of these last frontiers to filling my own holes is like being 50% better already. So instead of beating my Self up, I take a good look, do my best to understand why I am doing what causes imbalance, decide on which action to change in future events, and simply and kindly forgive my Self.

Many a time I've wondered, "Why," why can't I create overflow in my financial affairs? Why do I just get by? How much longer do I have to wait? What do I need to change? When will I finally have this all figured out? My closest friends would tell me that they are pretty tired of me saying why, what, and how—yet they do love the answers these questions have brought to the surface. It has sharpened my intuitive intelligence to a fine point and made me an expert in analyzing cause and effect. Today, all I have to do is look at any situation to see the blueprint of its creation, as well as what needs change to morph it into its most desired shape. I am so grateful for every Soul that has participated in bringing my true life's purpose to the surface, and I intend to lovingly polish and shine it for the rest of my life.

~

Fake it till you make it!

You have heard the expression "Fake it till you make it." Sitting on the couch and envisioning a promotion at work is a good start. To really bring the promotion into reality, you have to start taking action steps, even if they feel a bit awkward at first. Dress as if you already have the job, grab every opportunity to take on extra responsibilities that are part of the new job, take classes related to the skills required, and act as if you are already in charge.

Ask for an interview for the job even if it isn't available yet. List all the reasons why you are the person who is qualified and can do it best. You may not get the job at this particular firm, but don't be shocked if you hear about a possibly even more suitable one through someone you just met "randomly" at your sister's wedding.

Always ask that whatever you intend for your Self be for the Highest Good of all involved. This ensures that you bring creations and happenings into your life, which serve everyone who is affected by them and you know that something isn't meant to be if it doesn't work out. If what you aimed for doesn't work out, something better is waiting, usually right around the corner. This perspective allows you to move forward instead of putting your head in the sand when you come across an obstacle.

~

Truly discern between the different aspects of your inner voices. The Male voice in its most imbalanced form represents the Ego. The Ego voice is based on fear, and if you listen solely to your Ego voice, you experience being who you are not. On the opposite end, the Male voice leads you without direction, and this, too, creates undesirable results. The balanced Male voice is the one who comes up with clever plans. He does the math, uses his logic, his rationality, and is realistic in what can be done. The Female voice in its most balanced form represents the true Heart voice. She makes the initial choice based on how joyful a direction, idea, vision or dream feels, and helps the Male voice to create great results with the least effort. In her most imbalanced state, she is lazy, passive, and uses her creative juices for everyone but her Self. Your gut feeling, your instincts, your intuition, and your common sense will guide you to find what resonates with you well beyond the shadow of a doubt.

Above all, a true Wizard knows that he cannot pretend to be unaware of his own integrity, his own truth, and, therefore, always fully abides by his inner Knowing. He uses his magic to create greater results with less effort for the Highest Good of all, and has mastered his inner demons who pop up every so often to tempt him to use his abilities to gain wealth or status or to overpower those still innocent and pure.

Light is stronger than dark. When you open a door to a dark room, it is the light that streams in, not the dark that seeps out. Very little light can brighten up vast darkness. Are you still hiding in the dark, afraid of standing fully exposed in the brightness of light?

Living in luxury literally means living in the light. DO the Opus Lux, BE the proverbial light tower that shines the light for those who otherwise would be lost in the darkness, and be an extraordinary example for all who are ready to shed their heavy veils and create their own light.

Opus Lux Action Tip

Be happy when you see someone who has what you would like. The happier you are for them, the faster you manifest it for your Self. For a moment, look at the bigger picture and realize that all sentient Beings are animated by Creator energy, all of us are of the same Source, and are connected in more intricate ways than we consciously are aware of. Where do you start and where do I end? Looking at the other person, you could say, "I am having an interestingly different experience over there than I'm having over here, and I'm already experiencing what it feels like to have the success I would like to manifest in my physical reality, over there." You are having billions of experiences all at once, and the only thing that gives you the illusion of being separate, are the heavy veils that create the false image of isolation in our individual bodies. Our physical bodies are the vehicles that allow Higher Source to have as many different experiences as possible. Remember who you are: A Light-Being with a particular purpose and a perfect plan. Within you are all the answers to your questions, all solutions you may ever need, and the power to manifest everything you need to live your true life's mission. When you have trouble manifesting a particular goal, use body dowsing (explained in "Meridians – Pathways of Chi" on page 49) to tell you if you are on your true path. Stand up, hold your hands over your heart and ask if reaching the particular goal you are after, is important for the current unfolding of your life's calling. This will help you to focus on your true path and manifest all that is for your highest good with ease and grace.

Made in the USA
San Bernardino, CA
25 October 2012